OUR GIFTS

Identifying and Developing Leaders

David P. Mayer

Augsburg Fortress
Minneapolis

OUR GIFTS
Identifying and Developing Leaders

Developed in cooperation with the Division for Congregational Ministries of the Evangelical Lutheran Church in America, Michael R. Rothaar, project manager.

The "Personal Preferences" tool on pages 101-103 is adapted from *Shaping Ministry for Your Community*, copyright © 1993 Augsburg Fortress.

Scripture quotations are from New Revised Standard Version Bible, copyright © 1989 Division of Christian Education of the National Council of the Churches of Christ in the United States of America. Used by permission.

Series overview: David P. Mayer, Michael R. Rothaar
Editors: Laurie J. Hanson, Jill Carroll Lafferty

Cover design and series logo: Marti Naughton
Text design: James Satter
Cover photograph: Gordon Gray, FRPS

About the cover image: The centerpiece of the Resurrection Window in First Lisburn Presbyterian Church, Northern Ireland, was created by stained glass artist James Watson, Belfast, from fragments of church windows destroyed by a car bomb in 1981 and restored after a second bomb in 1989. The window symbolizes new life in Christ, which transforms darkness to light, hatred to love, despair to hope, and death to life. The members of First Lisburn Presbyterian have lived out this promise through new initiatives for community service, reconciliation, and peace-making.

ISBN 0-8066-4409-5

The paper used in this publication meets the minimum requirements of American National Standard for Information Sciences—Permanence of Paper for Printed Library Materials, ANSI Z329.48-1984.

Manufactured in the U.S.A.

06   05   04   03   02   1   2   3   4   5   6   7   8   9   10

✚ Contents

Series Overview

Welcome to the Congregational Leader Series, and welcome to the journey of discovering God's future for you and your congregation. Your congregation's mission and ministry are given to you by God. We sometimes refer to "our church," but it is always Christ's church. We are at best its stewards or caretakers, not its owners. As we plan, organize, and lead, we strive toward excellence in everything we do to reflect the glory and grace of God, who has entered human life to redeem us.

As a congregational leader, you may be asking, "What is our mission? How should we structure things? How can we plan for the future and where will the resources come from?" The Congregational Leader Series provides resources for effective planning and leadership development. Each book includes biblical and theological foundations for planning and leadership development, and practical information to use in building on your congregation's strengths.

We are first of all called to be faithful to God's word and will. Exploring the Bible enables us to discern what God's plan is for us as individuals and as a congregation. Ignoring or minimizing the centrality of God in our deliberations risks not only failure but also our faith. In the words of the psalmist, "Unless the LORD builds the house, those who build it labor in vain"(Psalm 127:1).

Why should we engage in congregational planning and leadership development? When the congregation is at its best, these activities aid us in fulfilling our mission to the world: reaching out with the gospel of Jesus Christ. Faithful planning for mission mirrors God's activity in the world, from creating and covenant-making to gathering and renewing the church. When congregations fail to plan, they risk dissipating the resources they have been given by God and begin falling away from all that God has intended for them.

In short, faithful planning and leadership development engage the congregation and all its members in the creative work of God. Continually analyzing and shaping our vision, mission, ministry, and context allows us to ask, "What is God calling our congregation to be?" Working to develop and support leaders enables us to ask, "How has God gifted each of us for ministry?"

We begin with prayer

As congregational leaders, we always begin our endeavors with prayer. Discerning God's will for us is a task that requires that we be in communication with God. Unfortunately, we often come up with new ideas and programs—and then pray that God will bless them! That order needs to be reversed. Our prayers should precede our plans, helping us discern God's call to us.

In his few years of public ministry, Jesus accomplished a tremendous amount of healing, teaching, and service for others. However, his ministry did not begin until after he had spent an extended period of time in the wilderness reflecting on his call and God's purpose for his life. Following that retreat, virtually every moment of his life's story was punctuated with prayer and ultimately concluded with his supplications in Gethsemane and on the cross.

Paul wrote to the Thessalonians, "Rejoice always, pray without ceasing, give thanks in all circumstances; for this is the will of God in Christ Jesus for you" (1 Thessalonians 5:16-18). These words were meant for us—congregational leaders anxious to get on with things that need to be done. Notice how Paul places *prayer* between *rejoice* and *thanks* in this verse. Prayer is not simply another task to be done nor an obligation to be met. It is a gift of God to be celebrated and used with joy and thanksgiving. It is meant to permeate our lives. As leaders, we are seeking to construct God's will in our communities. God invites us to build with gladness and to make prayer the mortar between every brick we lay.

As congregational leaders, we always begin our endeavors with prayer.

We build from strength

Most leadership resources begin with the assumption that there is a problem to be solved. In the midst of the real problems that surround us, however, our task as congregational leaders is to identify the strengths, giftedness, and blessings that God has given to us and the congregation. Our primary calling is not to be problem solvers but to be asset builders. Paul reminds us, "Let all things be done for building up" (1 Corinthians 14:26). This is not license to ignore problems, conflicts, or deficiencies. Rather, it is a call to view the brokenness around us in a new way.

Our primary calling is not to be problem solvers but to be asset builders.

Our role as Christian leaders is to attempt to look at our congregation, our fellow Christians, and ourselves, as God sees us. "This is my commandment, that you love one another as I have loved you" (John 15:12). Jesus did not blindly ignore the problems around him. Instead, he viewed those problems through a lens of love, appreciation, and forgiveness. We are called to build from strength, to construct our plans and visions from what God has given us. When we try to build from weakness and focus only on our problems, we compound both and ultimately fail.

First Church was located in a growing, well-to-do suburb, on a main thoroughfare, and in a beautiful new building. The members of First Church appeared to have everything going for them, and the congregation's future looked very bright.

The congregation, however, faced an ongoing problem with mortgage payments. This problem became so all-consuming that the congregation began to lose sight of its strengths, gifts, and mission for the future. The members of First Church had everything they needed to solve the problem of mortgage payments but they were unable to stop fixating on it. Soon, many other issues surfaced as everyone became a fault-finder.

Today there is no mortgage-payment problem because there is no First Church. The preoccupation with weakness and deficiency blinded the congregation to the reality of its gifts. This congregation died, not because of its problems but because of its perspective.

We must constantly ask ourselves and others, "Where is God at work here? What gifts have we received for ministry in this place?" Focusing only on what we don't have breeds jealousy, competition, hopelessness, and lost vision. Focusing on our gifts gives birth to joy, affirmation, and hope.

We won't find quick fixes

We live in a culture obsessed with quick fixes and mesmerized by the notion that there is a prescription for every ailment and accident. But things keep falling apart. People get sick. Programs fail. Committees don't function. Plans backfire. And goals aren't met. The list of mistakes, failures, misfires, and flops grows and grows. In his letter to the Romans, Paul reminds us that "all have sinned and fall short of the glory of God" (Romans 3:23). Paul says this not to weigh us down with despair, but instead to remind us that our salvation comes from God and not ourselves.

Faithful leaders have a deep respect for the reality of problems and obstacles. Things will always fall apart. That's why planning, assessing, goal-setting, leading, and visioning are ongoing processes, not quick fixes. As leaders, we need to know the nature of sin and publicly acknowledge its pervasiveness. Then we can lead, not with unhealthy fatalism, but with honesty, humility, and a sense of humor.

We are all ministers

As Christians, everything we do and plan is communal. We cannot plan unilaterally or devise strategies in isolation. To be sure, each of us has received salvation individually through baptism, but at that moment, through the water and the Word, we were united with the body of Christ. Even the gifts that God has given each of us are meant for the common good of all God's people: "To each is given the manifestation of the Spirit for the common good" (1 Corinthians 12:7).

In other words, each of us is a minister, whether pastor or lay person, and each of us is called to serve others. This is a radical departure from our culture's overwhelming emphasis on individual

Each of us is a minister, whether pastor or lay person, and each of us is called to serve others.

independence. The idea that we are all ministers and that as the church we minister as a community has tremendous implications for all of our planning and development efforts.

Leadership development is nothing more than equipping the members of the congregation so that they are strengthened for ministry: "The gifts he gave were that some would be apostles, some prophets, some evangelists, some pastors and teachers, to equip the saints for the work of ministry, for building up the body of Christ" (Ephesians 4:11-12). Paul would be appalled at the idea that a paid professional minister should carry out all of the ministry of the congregation or that only some people in the congregation are called to ministry.

Faithful planning and leadership development affirm that all of God's people are gifted and invited to participate in ministry. Identifying, embracing, and strengthening each other's gifts for common mission is a daunting task that never ends, but through that effort and in that journey we become what God intended: "But you are a chosen race, a royal priesthood, a holy nation, God's own people, in order that you may proclaim the mighty acts of him who called you out of darkness into his marvelous light" (1 Peter 2:9).

A model for understanding congregations

Congregations are extremely complex. Throughout the Congregational Leader Series, we invite you to look at your congregation through a particular model or set of lenses. This model helps us to understand why congregations are so complex, and it provides some important clues for the leadership skills and tasks that are needed.

A congregation resembles three different institutions at the same time: a *community of spiritual formation*, a *voluntary association*, and a *nonprofit organization*. This isn't a matter of size—the largest and smallest are alike in this. It isn't a matter of context—the model applies to both urban and rural settings. Each type of institution has different values and goals, which may even contradict each other. Each of these values and goals requires different things from leaders.

Communities of spiritual formation

A congregation is, in part, a community of spiritual formation. People come to such a community to join with others in growing closer to God. They seek to understand God's word and God's will for their life. They seek an experience of God's presence, a spiritual or emotional awareness of transcendence and love. They seek time for contemplation and prayer, and also time to work with others on tasks that extend God's love to others.

How are our congregations communities of spiritual formation? Much of congregational life centers on worship. We teach children and adults the practice of faith. The church provides support in Christ's name during times of crisis and need. We engage in visible and public activities, such as offering assistance to people who are homeless, or hungry, or survivors of abuse, as a way of both serving God and proclaiming God's mercy and justice.

The most important value in a community of spiritual formation is authenticity.

The most important value in a community of spiritual formation is authenticity. There is no room for pretense, no room for manipulation, and no room for power games. The goals we establish must be clearly directed to outcomes in people's spiritual lives. The fundamental question for self-evaluation is this: "How has our ministry brought people closer to God?"

Voluntary associations

Like any club or voluntary association, a congregation is a gathering of people who are similar to one another in specific ways, share a common purpose, and largely govern and finance their organization's existence and activities. In addition, people often find that belonging to a club is a way to make friends and social or business contacts, and enjoy meaningful leisure time activities. Some voluntary associations, such as Kiwanis or Lions clubs, have charitable purposes and sometimes seek support from people beyond their own membership. Some voluntary associations are focused on common interests or activities, such as gardening or providing youth athletic leagues.

Membership requirements may be strict or fluid, costs may be high or low, and commitments may be long or short, but they are spelled out rather clearly. A number of unwritten rules may serve to get people to conform to common values. Most voluntary associations would like to have more members, both to strengthen their organization and to expand the social benefits that come from a broader circle. But the new members usually are people who are very much like those who are already members.

The most important value in a voluntary association is effectiveness in helping people relate to one another.

The most important value in a voluntary association is effectiveness in helping people relate to one another. The goals are largely relational. There must be many opportunities for people to form relationships, especially with those with whom they have much in common. The association must operate in such a way that people all feel that their own values and hopes are being well served, usually through direct access to the decision-making process and ample opportunities for public dissent. People want and expect to be contacted regularly by both leaders and other members, and to feel that they are fully accepted as part of the group.

It is also important that there is a consensus—a shared vision—on what the association is and does. When conflict emerges, it must be negotiated and resolved. Because membership is voluntary, when there's conflict, or when they just don't feel part of the group anymore, people are usually quick to withhold their financial support or quit altogether.

Nonprofit organizations

As if it weren't complicated enough to be both a community of spiritual formation and a voluntary association, now consider that your congregation is also a nonprofit organization. It is a chartered or incorporated institution, recognized as a legal entity by the federal, state, and municipal government. A congregation can borrow and lend, sue and be sued. You as a congregation are accountable to society and responsible for following all applicable laws. Almost all congregations are property owners and employers. The congregation has formal operational procedures and documents (from your constitution to state laws) that dictate how you must make decisions and conduct your affairs. The usually unspoken but fundamental goal of a nonprofit organization is self-perpetuation, making sure that the institution will continue.

In this regard, congregations are similar to any business that offers services to the public. Being *nonprofit* simply means that the organization's assets can't be distributed to individuals or for purposes contrary to the charter. It doesn't mean that the congregation can't or shouldn't be run in a businesslike manner—or that it can't accumulate assets. The actual operation doesn't differ much from that of a profit-making business. In a nonprofit organization, the primary value is efficiency, or achieving the greatest results with the least possible expenditure of resources.

Another core value is continuity, with orderly systems that must be applied by anyone who carries out the organization's work. To reach financial goals, a nonprofit organization seeks voluntary contributions and often regularizes revenue through endowments and ancillary sources of income. Efforts are made to minimize costs without sacrificing quality. The organization also tries to build reserves to meet unanticipated circumstances and periodic needs (such as replacement of depreciating assets). Policies are in place to protect the staff and volunteers, and to ensure clear and mutually agreed upon expectations. There are clear lines of accountability and each person operates within a specified scope of decision-making.

Planning in a nonprofit organization includes making the best use of property and facilities. The property is seldom an end in itself, but the goal of leadership is always to maximize its usefulness. Other organizational goals revolve around having a truly public presence, including marketing effectively, identifying the needs and wants of a particular group of people, developing a product or service that addresses those needs, and informing the target group of its desirability and availability. Nonprofit organizations must do this as surely and skillfully as those in the profit sector.

In a nonprofit organization, the primary value is efficiency, or achieving the greatest results with the least possible expenditure of resources.

You may have heard that "you shouldn't be a manager, you should be a leader." This is unfortunate language, because management is part of leadership, and voluntary organizations need managers. How you analyze, organize, delegate, supervise, and evaluate the congregation's work is critical to its vitality.

Leadership

What does the word *leadership* really mean? Think of it as having three dimensions: *character, knowledge,* and *action. Character* permeates all three aspects of this model. Leaders have principles and try to live them out. In any of the three ways in which we're looking at congregations, leaders are honest, trustworthy, dedicated, caring, disciplined, and faithful to the core principles—and have many more virtues as well. Although everyone sins and fails, be clear that improvement is expected from all leaders.

It is not only character that counts. Leaders must also know things and do things. *Knowledge* and *action* can be developed. They can be learned in books and classes or from working with people who have expertise. Things we know from one part of our experience can be applied to other parts of our lives.

Applying the congregational model

The three-part model of congregations is helpful in exploring the different things that leaders must be, know, and do in a community of spiritual formation, in a voluntary association, and in a nonprofit organization.

Problems develop when the values, goals, and leadership styles appropriate to one part of the congregational model are mistakenly applied to one of the others. It is not wrong to value authentic spirituality, effective interpersonal relationships, and operational efficiency. There are times when each of these should be given the highest priority. Recognize that your congregation probably has emphasized one of these areas at the expense of the others, and plan your way to a better balance. Embrace the wonderful complexity of congregational life and ask God to move among us to change us and renew us and rededicate us to God's own purposes.

The Congregational Leader Series

This is one of several books in the Congregational Leader Series. The entire series seeks to build on the positive, basing your planning on assets rather than deficiencies, and to focus on outcomes, enabling your congregation to make a specific and definable difference in people's lives. The series has two sets: congregational planning and leadership development. Books in this series can be used in any order, so you can get started with those books that are most helpful for you and your congregation. The reproducible tools can be used with your council, committees, planning teams, leadership groups, and other members of the congregation. Visit www.augsburgfortress.org/CLS to download and customize these tools.

Faithful planning and leadership development take us on a journey, a pilgrimage, and an exploration of God's possibilities for you and your congregation. The Congregational Leader Series provides resources for your travels, as you seek God's will and guidance for you and your congregation.

This image of a cross indicates that further information on a topic appears in another book in the Congregational Leader Series.

Preface

This book is dedicated to Linda, Maggie, Louis, and Beverly:
my wife, daughter, father, and mother. They are my mentors
and my models of Christian leadership.

Throughout this resource you will find contemporary stories about individuals and groups involved in the leadership task. Sometimes the names and places have been changed, but the narratives are faithful to the events. I hope that these illustrations make this resource more real for you. Further, I encourage you to reflect on your own life's stories, and the stories of your congregation's members. Share these stories as you use this book. Your stories of past successes and joys will help bring your future efforts to life.

Enjoy!

Introduction

Our Gifts: Identifying and Developing Leaders is part of the Congregational Leader Series, which focuses on congregational planning and leadership development. This particular volume will explore lay leadership issues.

Overview

- Chapter 1 provides both an overview of some of the leadership issues and dilemmas facing your congregation, and a definition and description of Christian leadership.

- Chapters 2 and 3 focus on ways to develop a congenial atmosphere for identifying, recruiting, and developing leaders. These are the chapters that will help you create a congregational infrastructure and environment that will sustain your leadership development programs and events.

- Chapter 4 explores ministry in the church and world and the concept of giftedness. It offers practical tools for identifying members' gifts, skills, talents, and willingness to serve.

- Chapter 5 pays particular attention to your members' leadership styles. Knowing what motivates different people can improve your effectiveness in leadership training and volunteer matching. No two people are alike, and we overlook that truism at our own peril.

- Chapters 6 and 7 concentrate on recruiting, training, and supporting the leaders in your congregation.

- Chapter 8 is a collection of final thoughts and concluding remarks.

- A bibliography and a variety of diagnostic tools and self-study exercises are provided in the back of this book.

Is this for you?

This book is primarily designed for the professional staff and key leaders of your congregation. It is a guide for evaluating your existing leadership development efforts and a practical handbook of useable leadership strategies, programs, and tools.

Congregational leaders are tempted to look for the definitive answer or program that will solve their dilemmas. You will not find any quick fixes in this resource. You may find some helpful ideas, but you won't find any miraculous cures. What you will find are ways to rethink and restructure your congregation that can result in greater participation by the members. You will also find some ways of doing leadership development that are not only faithful to our traditions, but profoundly rewarding to those who participate. Be prepared to experience personal growth yourself as you take the lead in training and supporting others.

Identifying leaders and helping them to grow is not an easy task.

Identifying leaders and helping them to grow is not an easy task. Anyone who tells you it is has never attempted it, or is stretching the truth. This is a process with several steps:

- identifying individuals' gifts
- matching those gifts with real needs
- giving permission to those who want to try something new
- motivating others to accept new responsibilities
- faithfully training all the recruits for effectiveness
- providing them with a solid support system
- holding them accountable for their actions
- carefully evaluating their labors
- genuinely thanking them for a job well done

This process isn't easy, but it is incredibly rewarding. You will experience that reward when new people volunteer for old jobs, when new members bring new ideas, when discipleship is alive and thriving, and when a renewed sense of joy and celebration permeates the congregation.

Using this book

Several individuals and groups will find all or part of this book valuable:

- The pastor and professional staff
- The congregation council
- The Mutual Ministry Committee
- New member classes
- The Nominations Committee
- The Long-Range Planning Committee

After you have reviewed the material, decide how best to use it in your setting. Individually or in a group, use the checklists at the end of each chapter to answer the following questions:

- What is going well in our congregation? Do we act in ways that are consistent with the basic values and principles involved in this chapter?

- Based on this chapter, does our congregation have any areas for improvement or important responsibilities that are not being carried out at this time?

- How can we celebrate what is going well? What are the next steps to take in any areas for improvement or change?

All-day workshops or overnight retreats provide the greatest opportunities for building enthusiasm and motivation, while introducing the material in smaller segments over a greater period of time (such as in monthly council meetings) has the benefit of greater learning. By doing both, you will deepen participants' comprehension and their excitement for leadership development.

Chapter 1

The Leadership Dilemma

Congregations have a leadership dilemma. They are always looking for new leaders, individuals who will pick up the slack in the congregation's programs and ministries. They are looking for people who will serve on committees and task forces, and they are looking for new ways to revitalize those who are already serving. The process of recruiting and developing new leaders is at best difficult, and at worst nearly impossible.

Have you heard anyone on a Nominating Committee or congregation council say that leadership recruitment is akin to pulling teeth? Why don't more members willingly and enthusiastically volunteer for the critical tasks of your congregation? Exciting and faithful ministries are taking place in our churches; why don't more people get involved? What is it about the congregation and its members that makes this task so difficult?

Before proceeding to the answers to those questions, let's look at how a congregation functions.

Leadership in a typical congregation

A congregation is typically organized like a tall, narrow isosceles triangle (see illustration on page 19), with leadership at three different levels in the triangle. The pastor and the professional staff are commonly located at the top of the organization. The "leaders" of the congregation are on the second or middle level. At the bottom is the third and biggest level. This is where the overwhelming majority of the members are located.

In the typical congregation the upper level represents less than 1 percent of the organization's membership. The middle level is home to about 20 percent of the congregation and the lower level has 80 percent of the congregation's population. It is a truism, with more truth than fiction, that 20 percent of the members do 80 percent of the work. This truth is often reflected in the giving patterns of the congregation, where 20 percent or less of the members provide the great majority of the offerings. This is not the way that we would wish our congregations to function, but unfortunately it is what we have become.

The number of people in the top level of the organization rarely changes unless the congregation as a whole expands, necessitating the addition of staff. The percentage of people in the top level, however, stays the same or decreases. The middle level is occupied by those who see themselves as the dedicated minority who do the great majority of the church's work. This is probably where you find yourself. People in this middle level minority are usually the ones most concerned about the pastor burning out, their own overwork, and the difficulty of expanding the leadership pool. These are the people who read books like this one.

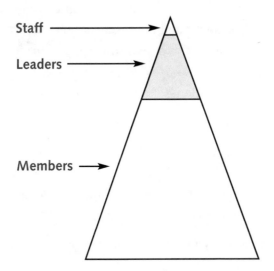

In the two top levels of this system reside the professional and volunteer leaders who sense both the inadequacy of this three-level system and the pressure to make it function for the mission of the gospel. The leaders might assume that the system's failure is the result of the apathy and immobility of the majority who are "hiding" in the third level. The overworked leaders cry out, "If only more people were involved! Why don't some of these people volunteer?" The unfortunate conclusion of the leaders caught in this system is that the congregation's biggest problem is the congregation's members.

The solution then becomes getting the nonparticipating members into the leadership level and allowing some of the present leaders to enjoy some well-deserved retreat and relaxation in the lower level. Unfortunately, this solution never expands the real number of individuals actively involved in the congregation's life. Ultimately, leadership recruitment becomes only a game of musical chairs, where there is no expansion of the leadership pool, and slowly but surely even the opportunities for service begin to disappear.

Three contemporary leadership myths

A wide variety of material dealing with leadership issues can be found in contemporary business and management literature. Much of this material is valuable, full of important information for business, but congregational leaders should be very cautious about some of the underlying leadership assumptions.

Three assumptions are among the more popular in contemporary literature on leadership:

1. Leaders are primarily problem solvers.

2. Leaders are primarily charismatic individuals who are often described as heroes and pioneers.

3. Leaders can solve any organizational problem using the natural laws of cause and effect.

These three assumptions pervade our culture and the church's understanding of leadership and organization. In fact, these assumptions are so pervasive that they have taken on almost mythical proportions. Unfortunately, they have little to do with how a pastor or congregational leader should function in the Christian community. When we embrace these assumptions we do it at the expense of the biblical record and our theological understandings of leadership.

Myth 1: Leaders are primarily problem solvers

The pastor, like any leader in the congregation, is called to be primarily a question asker and not an answer giver. In business the leader tells her subordinates what to do to solve a problem. In the congregation the leader asks, "What is the faithful thing to do in this situation?" In contemporary society, leaders are expected to have the answers to all the problems. In the church, leaders are preoccupied with questions: Where is God at work in this congregation? Where is the Spirit calling us? How have we been gifted for ministry?

Pastors and leaders focus on God's activity among God's people. This is often in stark contrast to our everyday fixation on what is not happening, what is not going right, and what we don't have. This is not to suggest that pastors and congregational leaders are called to ignore problems—they would have to be particularly naive to think that sin does not abound. Rather, pastors and leaders are called to pay attention to what they want to see grow: faith, community, service, holiness, prayer, justice, and the many other gifts of God. When pastors and leaders ask questions about these things, the congregation comes alive.

Pastors and leaders focus on God's activity among God's people.

Myth 2: Leaders are primarily charismatic individuals

The second leadership myth states that leaders are individuals with strong personal styles and goals who are called to bend systems, issues, and organizations to their will. In contrast, pastors and congregational leaders are called to lead communally as servants. Pastors are not called to heroically and brilliantly perform all the ministry tasks of the church. They are called to preach and teach in such a way that all of God's people are strengthened and encouraged for ministry. Through the office of Word and Sacrament the pastor speaks of and demonstrates God's way of leading. This way of leading calls on all of the baptized to empty themselves on behalf of others, and to work communally within a body whose ultimate leader is Christ.

Myth 3: Leaders can solve any organizational problem

The third contemporary leadership myth assumes that systems and organizations function somewhat like machines, and that the modern leader is the equivalent of a mechanic. When the organization is not functioning well the leader refers to the owner's manual, makes the necessary adjustments, and then stands back to observe the beneficial effects of the adjustment. If the organization persists in operating poorly, other observations and adjustments are made. The leader in this model is responsible for reading all of the latest owner's manuals and mechanical journals, and for diagnosing the organization's needs.

The congregation is not a machine but an incredibly complex organism.

Anyone who has worked in a congregation, or any other volunteer organization, knows that this third assumption is indeed a myth. The congregation is not a machine that reliably responds to our tune-ups. The complexity of human interactions in a Christian community, combined with the reality of sin and brokenness, make our attempts at mechanical adjustment look foolish and futile. The congregation is not a machine but an incredibly complex organism. Like a plant, you can put the seed in the ground, water it, give it sunlight and fertilizer, but you cannot predict how many leaves, flowers, roots, or thorns the seed will generate. We can approximate the outcome but we cannot predict it. Because of this we should not expect our pastors and leaders to be able to change our congregations with great speed and simple programs.

The leadership of the apostles

The Acts of the Apostles in the Bible is a rich digest of the earliest years of the church. It is also a rich source for understanding the nature and function of the church and its leadership. It may not offer an exact blueprint for leadership recruitment and development, but it does provide some extremely important themes and guidelines. The leaders who inhabit the book of Acts give us a wonderful, human, and faithful picture of a church functioning without the three levels of leadership described in this chapter.

One of the best and most disconcerting descriptions of the leadership of the apostles is found in Acts 4:13: "Now when they saw the boldness of Peter and John and realized that they were uneducated and ordinary men, they were amazed and recognized them as companions of Jesus." As early church leaders, Peter and John were not known for their intellectual superiority or even their charismatic qualities, but for their bold witness to Jesus Christ. What a striking contrast to our contemporary expectations that leaders show their superiority in intellectual mastery, problem analysis, and organizational diagnosis!

In Acts we also see that the three levels of leadership in a congregation did not yet exist: "Now the whole group of those who believed were of one heart and soul, and no one claimed private ownership of any possessions, but everything they owned was held in common" (Acts 4:32). The early ideal of the church, reflecting the teaching of Jesus and the theology of Paul, was communal. Consensus rather than competition was the preferred style. The common good was the goal, not the individual's elevation. Actions that celebrated individualism were punished when they occurred, as in the case of Ananias and Sapphira (Acts 5:1-11).

See the "Leadership Bible Study" tool on pages 87-88 for more on leadership and the book of Acts.

The Holy Spirit's presence

The qualities of leadership that were sought out and recognized by the early church were almost always linked to the presence of the Holy

Spirit. It has been suggested the Acts of the Apostles should more accurately be called "The Acts of the Holy Spirit." Paul in his letters often provides us with lists of the gifts of the Spirit and the fruits of the Spirit, but in Acts we are able to read about those gifts in action.

In the book of Acts, the presence of the Holy Spirit is what makes a leader. The characteristics of a leader filled with the Holy Spirit are faith, boldness, and joy. The Holy Spirit is manifested in many other ways such as in miracles and speaking in tongues. Yet these manifestations always emerge out of a context where the leaders have the courage of their convictions to act and speak with gladness for what Christ has done.

The story of one Christian leader

Standing in front of a coffin in a funeral home is always an awkward and humbling experience. Fred, a member of our congregation, had died unexpectedly. He was my age, and that fact added a degree of gravity to the moment.

I introduced myself to Fred's son, Don, whom I had never met. His response surprised and warmed me. "Dad loved your congregation and the members. You know, when he moved to town, he had just been divorced and was suffering from years of alcoholism. After he joined your congregation all that changed. He never took another drink. Zion Lutheran saved his life. Thank you."

I was very glad that our congregation had a major impact on Fred's life. I was even more pleased to look back and see that Fred had not merely been a "pew sitter," but had served on the congregation council and numerous committees and had frequently put his writing and other skills to work on behalf of the congregation and its ministry.

When Fred arrived in town he was a very unlikely candidate for congregational leadership. Nothing in his past predicted that he would be an active and willing leader.

In this book, a Christian *leader* is someone who is called by God and the church to grow in his or her faith and to courageously and joyfully share that faith with others through word and action. In the next chapter we will discuss this definition of leadership in more detail and look at what it means to be a *disciple-leader*.

Checklist

❏ Our congregation functions like the triangle with three levels, and is seeking to change.

❏ Our pastor is not primarily a problem solver for our congregation.

❏ More than 20 percent of our congregation's members have active leadership roles.

❏ Our leadership works at developing consensus rather than voting or competition.

❏ We have many "Freds" in our congregation.

❏ We regularly discuss biblical models for leadership recruitment and development.

Chapter 2

The Disciple-Leader

A Christian leader is someone who is called by God and the church to grow in his or her faith and to courageously and joyfully share that faith with others through word and action.

This is a challenging definition and description of a Christian leader. It assumes that leaders are constantly growing. It also assumes that congregations are willing to constantly teach and encourage their members to grow in the faith. In short, this definition calls on congregations to act as discipling communities, and calls on members and leaders to see themselves as disciples. In this chapter we will discuss what it means to be a *disciple-leader* and the congregational tasks that will encourage and strengthen members for that role.

The word *disciple* means student, pupil, or learner. In the New and Old Testaments the word *disciple* is usually connected with a particular prophet, teacher, or rabbi. We are most familiar with the disciples of Jesus, his close circle of 12 apprentices and a larger group of followers. These people were Jesus' students. In a sense they were members of the Jesus School. They had only one teacher, who had invited them to follow him.

Continually growing in faith

When Jesus' ministry began none of the disciples were capable of fulfilling the role of a leader. Like you and me, the disciples of Jesus were not born leaders. They needed to be taught, mentored, and sent out on their own to teach and heal before they would become leaders. After three years with their teacher, and by the power and inspiration of the Holy Spirit, those 12 disciples were prepared to assume the responsibilities of leadership. This process of learning and growing in the faith never stopped. Even after Pentecost, the disciples continued their faith journey. They became known as apostles or messengers, but they remained disciple-leaders, continuing to learn and struggle and grow in the faith.

That same process is true for us. As modern disciple-leaders we never finish growing in the faith. In the church we are never simply leaders, those special people who are in charge of things. Instead, all members are potential leaders and apprentices to Jesus. As a disciple-leader every baptized member is called to continually mature in his or her faith.

Similarly the congregation is called to make disciple-leaders of its members, teaching and strengthening everyone so that they grow in faith and are given the courage and joy to share their faith in word and action. This task is never fully completed. The congregation and all its members need to see that they are on a journey of disciple-leader development. The congregation and its members are never done growing. They are spiritual pilgrims, always traveling to a new territory and always learning new things about their faith.

The congregation and all its members are on a journey of disciple-leader development.

Where the journey begins

In the church, recruiting and developing leaders is the process of recruiting and developing disciples. The call to discipleship is extended in baptism and confirmed and nurtured through the church. That process emerges out of the worship of the congregation. Preaching the Word and celebrating the sacraments are the focal points for recruiting disciple-leaders. At each worship service, we should extend an invitation to people to come and see who Jesus is, and to come and taste a new life in Christ. Ideally, this invitation forms the center of the congregation's life, and provides the arena for recruiting and developing new disciples. If your congregation is already extending this invitation, you are well on your way to infusing new life into your leadership development efforts. During the preaching and the prayers, simple reminders of our communal call to discipleship can infuse new life into tired leaders and inspire action in those who have not yet seen themselves as disciple-leaders.

Disciple-leaders are not born; they are shaped and molded. That molding process happens within the Christian community and is empowered by the Holy Spirit. Disciple-leaders are formed through the means of grace, prayer, Bible study, and fellowship. This process of making disciple-leaders is the same today as it was when the church began: "They devoted themselves to the apostles' teaching and fellowship, to the breaking of bread and the prayers" (Acts 2:42).

Disciple-leaders are not born; they are shaped and molded.

Setting the tone

Most congregations need to begin the process of developing disciple-leaders by retooling their existing organizational structures. That process begins with the congregation council and other leadership groups and committees (deacons, trustees, and so on). Your present congregational leaders set the organizational tone and provide the model for the rest of the members.

Every meeting of the congregation council should begin with prayer followed by a group discussion that is focused on a part of scripture. All members of the council should be encouraged to participate in the discussion. As the relationships between council members mature, the group should be encouraged to venture into discussions related to each other's personal growth in faith.

Growing Together: Spiritual Exercises for Church Committees, by Rochelle Melander and Harold Eppley, is an excellent book full of useful topics for aiding congregation councils on their disciple-shaping journey. *Growing Together* contains 50 opening exercises that include prayers, discussion starters, and Bible studies.

See *Growing Together: Spiritual Exercises for Church Committees.*

Topics for group prayer, Bible study, and discussion could include:

• Disciple-leaders in the book of Acts

• What does it mean to be "called"?

• Paul's advice for congregations in 1 Corinthians

• Prayer in the New Testament and today

• Sinful leaders: Moses, David, Jonah, and Paul

• Communion and community in Scripture

See the "Leadership Bible Study" tool on pages 87–88 for other topics. These topics can be handled either in one meeting or as a series that is used over a period of time.

Expanding the process

The process of reshaping the congregation's structure for leadership development should next be expanded to all of the congregation's committees and task forces. Again, the previous list of topics and the book *Growing Together* can provide some helpful discussion starters and questions for reflection and discussion.

Initially, some committees and perhaps the congregation council may object to giving up their valuable time for community and disciple building. Actually, this will add little or no time to the agenda. The following sample agenda could be used for any committee or group meeting:

• Opening prayer: 1 minute

• Scripture reading and discussion: 10 minutes

• Personal sharing of joys and concerns: 10 minutes

• Business meeting: 60-65 minutes

• Closing prayer intercessions: 5 minutes

The prayer, Bible study, and discussion can provide a lens that helps focus the work of the group and sharpen its vision for ministry. In the final analysis, your congregation's organizational structure will begin to function more like a community than a committee, and your leaders will begin to see themselves as disciples of the faith and not merely as organizational bureaucrats "doing their duty."

Once the existing leaders and committee members have begun to experience and welcome this new style, then the process should be expanded to all groups and auxiliaries in the congregation. The choirs, youth groups, new member classes, confirmation and Sunday school classes, and other organizations can easily assimilate the components

---

The Growth Group

In 1975 I had the privilege of helping to start a small-group ministry in my home congregation, Trinity Lutheran Church. The pastor and I simply invited anyone who wanted to grow in faith to come to an informational meeting. Eight people responded. Some were active members of the church. Several were not.

We met monthly for prayer, faith sharing, and far-ranging discussions of contemporary theology. The essays of Paul Tillich and the life of Francis of Assisi inspired some particularly memorable discussions. The personal sharing time matured steadily as we encouraged each other in our faith journeys.

The Growth Group lasted about a year before disbanding, but its effects are still felt today. Those who had been active members of the congregation expanded their activity. Those who had been inactive became heavily involved in the congregation and community. During the life of the group, the members organized countless service projects for people in need. One group member was inspired to write a new curriculum for the Sunday school and another member began the first senior citizens organization in town. Those initiatives continued to thrive for many years. The Growth Group gave all of its members the content and the courage to share their faith in word and action.

of prayer, Bible study, and fellowship into their time together. Opportunities for developing as disciple-leaders need to be provided to all members, but particular attention should be given to children and youth. Raising up our youngest members in the disciplines of the church ensures that our leadership development efforts are long-term.

Building Christian community

Disciple-leaders cannot develop in isolation. They need Christian communities like the Growth Group to recruit them, nurture them, teach them, send them, and hold them accountable. Congregations that are anxious to expand their leadership must vigorously expand the opportunities for communal fellowship. The sense of belonging and the presence of the sacred that are found in Christian community not only build up disciples in our congregations but also provide an extremely attractive alternative culture for those who are not church members.

Disciple-leaders cannot develop in isolation.

Serious attempts to recruit and support congregation leaders require the development of ministries or communities where faith can be practiced and strengthened in a caring environment. Leadership workshops and training events alone cannot provide this. These events, which we have tended to rely upon in the past, are heavily task-oriented. They are valuable tools for sharing intellectual under-standings and introducing new skills, but without community build-ing components they cannot provide essential dynamics for attracting and developing disciples.

Small-group ministries

Small groups comprised of no more than eight members each can provide the relational dimensions and the communal environment for developing Christian leaders and disciples.

To be effective in developing disciple-leaders, seek to involve at least 30 to 40 percent of the congregation's members in small-group ministries. In most cases, retooling your existing committees and groups will result in 20 percent involvement. Initiating a variety of new small groups will help you achieve or exceed 40 percent involvement overall. Use the following formula to find out the number of small groups to initiate in your congregation to reach a goal of 40 percent involvement.

A. Fill in the number of active members in your congregation.

B. Fill in the number of members on committees or task forces.

C. Fill in the number of members in existing groups such as choirs, youth groups, new member classes, confirmation and Sunday school classes, and other organizations.

D. Add B and C together to obtain the total number of members involved in existing committees and groups.

E. Calculate the number of people needed to reach 40 percent involvement by multiplying A by 0.4.

F. Subtract D from E to obtain the number of additional people needed to reach 40 percent involvement. (If D is equal to or greater than E, 40 percent involvement has been achieved in your congregation. Consider setting a new goal for involvement.)

G. Using an average of 8 members per group, obtain the number of small groups needed to expand involvement to 40 percent by dividing F by 8.

	Example	Your Congregation
Number of active members	A. 300	_____
Number of members on committees	B. 30	_____
Number of members in existing groups	C. 30	_____
Add B and C	D. 60	_____
Multiply A by 0.4	E. 120	_____
Subtract D from E	F. 60	_____
Divide F by 8	G. 7.5	_____

The example shows that a congregation of 300 active members that presently functions with three levels will need to start between seven and eight small groups in order to expand its pool of disciple-leaders to 40 percent of the congregation.

Small-group ministries are not a fad, a quick fix program, or a short-term solution to a long-term problem. Small groups or Christian communities have been the source of reformation and renewal in the church throughout history. It all began in the house churches of the early Christians (Acts 20:20), and has been duplicated by each succeeding generation. What we call small-group ministry has also been called monasticism, Methodist classes, the Catholic Worker Movement, religious orders, and pietism. Regardless of title, each of these Christian communities brought about great renewal and revival in the church.

Beginning a small-group ministry

If you choose to begin a small-group ministry in your congregation, there are some important first steps. First, be sure that the entire congregation is aware of your new initiative. Use the congregation's Sunday bulletin, newsletter, and information meetings for introducing small-group ministry. Cottage meetings, using a small-group ministry model, have been particularly helpful in sharing information and gaining recruits. If your congregation hasn't done anything like this before, take the time to provide some workshops on the background of small-group ministry. Some of the workshop topics could be:

Be sure that the entire congregation is aware of your new initiative.

• The history of Christian communities
• Learning to pray together
• The Christian disciplines
• How to lead a committee or small group
• Turning committees into communities

Second, initial training for your small-group leaders is essential. Whether they are committee chairpersons already in office or new small-group leaders, provide some basic information and opportunities for skills development. This can be done by training all your leaders in a workshop or by putting new leaders into existing groups with experienced leaders. Ongoing leadership training and support can be provided by the pastor, professional staff, a committee (small group!), or a small-group ministry coordinator. Whether you are starting a small-group ministry or turning committees into communities, the book *Starting Small Groups—and Keeping Them Going* by George S. Johnson, David Mayer, and Nancy Vogel (Augsburg Fortress, 1995, ISBN 0-8066-0125-6) has numerous resources for planning and implementing your congregation's program. Using this book or a similar resource in your training and support will provide consistency within all your groups and give your group leaders a common language and methodology.

Third, small groups need regular oversight. Oversight by the pastor, staff, or small-groups coordinator ensures that the various small groups stay tightly connected to the whole congregation. Without oversight, small groups can begin to develop into divisive cliques or enclaves. Many small-group experts suggest regularly splitting up (multiplying) small groups or limiting the duration of their existence. Designing a small-group covenant that outlines mutual expectations for confidentiality, membership, and the time frame is also highly recommended. Your goal is to recruit and strengthen disciple-leaders for your entire congregation. Oversight and mutually understood accountabilities can make that happen.

Remember that Christian leaders are people who joyfully share their faith.

Finally, have fun! Remember that Christian leaders are people who joyfully share their faith. Growing, learning, and maturing as a disciple-leader should be a joyful process. Small groups and transformed committees should be places that we are excited about joining. Relax, share, listen, and let the Holy Spirit work in the lives of those gathered. Christian community is not a problem to be solved, but a gift of God to be enjoyed, celebrated, and cherished.

In the next chapter we will discuss the ways in which your entire congregation—even the members who don't want to participate—can be involved in identifying, recruiting, and strengthening disciple-leaders.

Checklist

❑ Our congregation sees leadership recruitment and development as a long-term process.

❑ We expect our leaders to constantly grow in faith.

❑ We provide numerous opportunities to help our members to grow in discipleship.

❑ Our committees function as communities that emphasize relation-ships as well as tasks.

❑ We have the optimum number of small groups for our congrega-tion's size.

❑ Committee membership is a joy, and recruiting members is not too difficult.

❑ Prayer, Bible study, and personal sharing are regular parts of all our congregation's functions, organizations, and groups.

Chapter 3

How to Mobilize Everyone

"This congregation has no leaders!" Imagine the effect if you made that announcement on a Sunday before worship. Those who are leaders in the congregation would be offended. Those who have thought about leading would now not be so sure, and the rest of the congregation would be wondering why you are so negative. The ultimate effect of such an announcement would be self-fulfilling. The congregation would lose its leaders.

Now, imagine the opposite. Before worship you announce, "Everyone in this congregation is a leader!" Following that announcement, not everyone would volunteer to lead, but they would know that expectations are very high for every member in the congregation. Some individuals who never thought of themselves as leaders would begin to think otherwise. The self-image of the congregation and its members would begin to change.

The power of what we think and say

What we think about and what we say shapes our reality. Theologically speaking, the Word has incredible power to shape us and our environment. When the words, "I now pronounce you husband and wife" are said, a new reality breaks in. When Jesus announced that the kingdom of God had come near, the cosmos shifted. The same is true for you and me. Our words and imaginings create new realities. It is not magic or even miraculous. What we think and talk about become life and reality. If, as a pastor or leader, I am convinced that my congregation has no potential disciple-leaders, then it is highly unlikely that I will ever identify and recruit new people. However, if I believe and say that my congregation is full of leaders, leaders will begin to emerge.

The Pygmalion effect

The phenomena known as the Pygmalion effect comes from a series of experiments done in school classrooms. Teachers were told that some of their students were bright, creative, and hard-working. They were also told that other students were not bright, tended to do poorly, and were not well-behaved. You can imagine the results. Teachers taught students according to the images they had been given. The students performed to the teachers' expectations, regardless of their abilities and past performance. Because of the negative effects on some of the students, these experiments have been discontinued. The Pygmalion studies dramatically illustrated the power that personal images play in development.

When teaching children to ride a bike, hit a baseball, or sing a song, we say, "You can do it!" When bowling we tell ourselves to roll a strike. Both of these images and encouragements increase the likelihood of success. We bring on the opposite result when we nervously tell a child not to fall off a bike. When we tell ourselves not to throw the bowling ball in the gutter, we preoccupy our mind with images of failure.

If we want to mobilize everyone in the church for leadership, we need to speak and to act in ways that say, "Everyone in this congregation is a disciple-leader." To think and to say anything less is to guarantee less. Furthermore, it is essential that we believe what we say, and do not simply engage in sloganeering about leadership in order to gain recruits.

> Everyone in this congregation is a disciple-leader.

System-wide re-imagining

Developing an affirmative atmosphere where all members begin to see themselves as disciple-leaders takes time, energy, and a wide variety of tools. Making a positive announcement before worship is great, but it will not change the congregation's environment. Likewise, an announcement in the bulletin will change few minds.

A system-wide strategy is necessary to create long-term and lasting change.

Changing your congregation's self-image and its reality takes constant repetition of affirming messages in a wide variety of media. A system-wide strategy is necessary to create long-term and lasting change. You've already begun that approach by retooling your committees, starting a small-groups ministry, and redefining leadership in your congregation (see chapters 1 and 2). Now you need to help the entire congregation to re-imagine itself as a congregation of fully engaged disciple-leaders. What follows are a number of programs and processes that can be woven together for system-wide re-imagining in your congregation. These processes and programs should be carefully adapted to fit the particular needs and context of your congregation.

Appreciative Inquiry

Appreciative Inquiry is an organizational development process that was developed by David Cooperrider in 1986. At the heart of Appreciative Inquiry (AI) is an interview process that gets everyone in the system talking about the high points and strengths of their organization. Most congregations are familiar with questionnaires and group discussions that focus on the congregation's problems. *That is not AI!* AI views the organization as a miracle to be appreciated and nurtured, not as a problem to be solved.

An unreservedly positive interview guide is developed and used with individuals and groups to elicit stories about best practices and preferred futures. (For an example, see the "Appreciative Inquiry Interview Guide" on pages 89-91.) The AI theory emphasizes building from strength, and creating an organizational atmosphere where all participants are engaged in thinking and talking about affirmative options for the future. As with the Pygmalion effect, AI raises positive expectations in the community that result in more positive outcomes.

Begin introducing AI in your congregation by naming a steering committee of five to eight people. Together study the "Appreciative Inquiry Interview Guide" on pages 89-91. Once the group has familiarized itself with AI theory and process, begin to develop your own protocols and interview guide.

The key to AI effectiveness is involving the greatest possible number of people in the interview process. These interviews can be done in small groups or individually. Frequent announcements to the congregation about AI and your process should precede the interviews by at least six weeks. The congregation has never done anything like this before, so significant information is essential in advance. Highlighting the positive affirming qualities of AI will dispel some of the members' concerns about being interviewed.

Invite everyone, including young people, to sign up for an interview. Provide many different days and times as options for the interviews. (This reduces the potential for people to claim they couldn't find the time to participate.)

> Invite everyone, including young people, to sign up for an interview.

The steering committee should practice AI by interviewing one another, and then training others to help facilitate the conversations. Interviewers should take notes during the interviews and pay particular attention to life-giving stories, new insights, and the "grace notes" of the conversation.

Following the interviews, the steering committee collects the data and shares it with the entire congregation. This can be done in a special presentation, at a church dinner, in a booklet that highlights some of the more exciting stories, or in any other fashion that excites the group's imagination. Retelling the best stories of the past and the most creative dreams of the future helps to flesh out new realities for the congregation. Retelling the story of the time when everyone pitched in to build a new addition to the church awakens memories of past glory and raises the congregation's desire to do something like that again.

The steering committee then studies the interview data carefully and uses the results to shape new actions and programs for the future. Recommendations from the committee should be acted upon by the congregation council, shared with the congregation, and implemented as soon as possible. When members see their ideas and interview responses being acted upon, congregational momentum and anticipation accelerate. (To implement an AI process in your congregation, see the "Appreciative Inquiry Planning Process" tool on pages 92-94.)

Organizing an AI process takes time and patience. Some members will have difficulty with an interview that is only positive and upbeat. Taking the time to explain the rationale of AI will pay great dividends. Encouraging members to save their problems, issues, and negative comments for another time will ensure a process that builds upon assets and strengths.

The use of AI in the congregation is limited only by your imagination. In order for AI to be a successful and effective process you only need to keep a few things in mind: look constantly for the best in the congregation and its members, be flexible and open to surprise, and have fun. AI is a joyful experience that ought to be contagious.

Volunteer recognition events

Publicly thanking and recognizing those members of the congregation who provide leadership today is essential. Volunteer recognition events will encourage those who serve and can inspire others to

---

In addition to the questions in the "Appreciative Inquiry Interview Guide" on pages 89-91, you may want to try some of these:

- Tell me a story about a time when you really felt like you were ministering in daily life.

- What are some things that would help you be the kind of disciple-leader that God wants you to be?

- Who was the finest leader you have ever known? What made that person great?

- What three leadership qualities do you wish you had? Why?

- Tell me a story about a time when you were asked to take leadership in something and you jumped right in. What excited you about that opportunity?

volunteer. When done well, these events celebrate God's work among us and remind us that we are all called to discipleship. Recognition events give life to many of the things we hear about in an Appreciative Inquiry.

A volunteer recognition event should be a special event, a cross between a birthday party and an honors banquet. This special event could be held in conjunction with a congregation's annual meeting, if that means an increase in participation. If not, pick another time or occasion. In the midst of the celebration invite the Sunday school superintendent to come forward and honor all the teachers and teachers' aides. Recognize the oldest member. Celebrate the youngest member. Ask all the quilters to stand up. Make sure you thank all of the council and committee members. Use this as a time to highlight new ministries and new ministers. A Ministry in Daily Life Award(s) could be presented. The list of possibilities is almost endless.

A recognition event should celebrate and demonstrate both the quality and quantity of disciple-leaders who are already serving. Don't overlook the youth and their contributions or the congregation's elders and their years of service. Not everyone can be recognized and honored, but everyone should be excited about what has taken place in the past, the number of individuals who have made those things happen, and the opportunities for service in the coming year.

> A recognition event should celebrate and demonstrate both the quality and quantity of disciple-leaders.

Ministry in daily life

The church exists not for its own sake but for the sake of the world. Many of the members of your congregation know this, and are active as leaders and ministers in their daily lives. Like the volunteers in the congregation, these people are not often recognized for their service in the community. Making the connection between faith and daily life can be difficult, and when it happens those moments and ministers need to be recognized.

A Ministry in Daily Life Sunday, perhaps on Labor Day weekend, is a wonderful way to make those elusive connections between church and world, Sunday and weekday. This is also a great opportunity to once again focus on disciple-leadership and our communal call to service. Some congregations invite everyone to come to this special Sunday worship wearing the same clothes that they wear Monday through Friday. If your congregation is a little too homogeneous to make this interesting, have everyone bring a symbol or sign of what they do every day and place those offerings before the altar. This imagery awakens us to the incredible variety of ministries and service that take place in daily life.

Celebrating those people who are serving in daily life gives them new energy and awakens new possibilities in the minds and hearts of others. Services such as the Affirmation of Baptism in the Lutheran Book of Worship can be used to help focus congregation members on their shared call to ministry. Temple talks, chancel dramas, and thematic preaching can be used to affirm or encourage members to continue serving others or to take new steps in that direction.

Commissioning leaders

Almost every congregation installs its new council members and some install Sunday school teachers on rally day. It often stops there. Congregations seeking to make system-wide, long lasting changes in identifying and developing leaders should commission or install virtually every new leader and volunteer. Use or adapt rites such as the "Installation of Elected Parish Officers" and "Recognition of Ministries in the Congregation" in Occasional Services: A Companion to Lutheran Book of Worship frequently to bless and send out new leaders.

Commission or install virtually every new leader and volunteer.

Why not install committees and special task forces (such as the AI Steering Committee), and recognize nursery attendants, after school volunteers, the quilting group, conference attendees, and home visitors? Each of these and many others are unique and valuable ministries. Those who serve in these ministries are disciple-leaders. Each time we commission and send out new ministers we affirm the Holy Spirit's work among us and invite others to participate.

Be open to surprise

In the Acts of the Apostles a disagreement arose among the disciples about who would distribute the food to the widows among them (Acts 6:1-6). The Hellenists felt slighted and the apostles felt overworked. The entire community decided that they needed to commission some Spirit-filled members to take over the ministry of food distribution. Seven new leaders were selected for the task, including Stephen.

However, in Acts 6:8 we read, "Stephen, full of grace and power, did great wonders and signs among the people." There is no record that Stephen ever served a single meal or delivered food to anyone, but there is abundant testimony that he did mighty acts of faith and courage. In the end Stephen became the church's first martyr.

The early church in its wisdom was open to the surprise of the Holy Spirit, and did nothing to quench its movement or Stephen's initiative. There is no record that the apostles told Stephen to quit doing his powerful signs and wonders. No one said, "Get back to serving tables like you're supposed to."

This story reminds us that we need to constantly open ourselves to surprises and guard against limiting and curtailing the Spirit's activity in our midst. When we begin to work at raising up disciple-leaders, we need to also be ready to give permission to those who would do things that we don't expect or plan.

The early church in its wisdom was open to the surprise of the Holy Spirit.

Constant communication

Some congregations have found it helpful to recognize a "Minister of the Month" in their church newsletter. These cameo pieces can focus on ministry in daily life or leadership and service in the church.

Ideally, these ministry snapshots describe individuals who have connected their service in the church and in the community. Whether
you use the congregation's newsletter, Sunday bulletin, narthex bulletin board, or all of the above to recognize a Minister of the Month,
make sure that the picture you paint is of someone who is just like
every other member of the congregation. Give the members of your
congregation pictures and examples that they can relate to, not images
and ideals that are unattainable.

Constantly communicate the importance of individual disciple-
leaders in the life of the church. Does your congregation's newsletter
list all of the members who are serving on committees and task forces?

Pam's Story

Pam was a very quiet and thoughtful member of St. John's Lutheran Church. Single
and in her 30s, she was a successful accountant who helped with the bookkeeping at
the church. Pam was the kind of person who was always around, very dependable, and
seldom noticed by others.

One Sunday I sat with Pam during worship. We shared a few pleasantries during the
prelude and shared the peace when invited. Like everyone else, I didn't know her very
well. I was both surprised and uncomfortable when, toward the end of worship, she
began to cry. She cried a lot. Something had really touched Pam.

I asked her if she was all right. "I'm fine," she replied, as she sniffled and blew her
nose. I pushed on, "Is something wrong?" Pam explained, "Didn't you hear? The pastor just prayed for me and gave thanks for me . . . and I'm not even sick."

I realized that during the prayers of the church, one of the petitions had named a number of people and given thanks to God for their ministry in the church and the world.
No one had ever publicly prayed for Pam by name and the effect was profound. Pam's
tears were tears of joy and gratitude. The pastor continued the practice for a number of
weeks and others were similarly touched.

Does the Sunday bulletin list the staff members and recognize all the members of the congregation as ministers? Are thank-you notes and public recognition given to those who complete ministry tasks in the congregation and community? Do you pray for others and their ministries by name even when they are not ill, grieving, or in the hospital? Does your stewardship campaign lift up the ministries that are happening and the disciple-leaders who are serving? The opportunities for communicating stories about leadership are endless.

Encouraging potential leaders

Mobilizing everyone for disciple-leadership cannot be accomplished with any single program. It takes system-wide change—changing what we think about, what we talk about, and what we do. Everyone in your congregation is a disciple-leader, but they may not know that. It is our job to tell them that in a hundred different ways throughout the year.

Those who aren't actively involved in the life of your congregation are not problem people. They are potential leaders needing encouragement, affirmation, and a new vision of who they are as God's people called to serve.

> Those who aren't actively involved in the life of your congregation are not problem people.

Checklist

❏ Our congregation recognizes and celebrates our members' ministries in all of our printed materials.

❏ We have a plan for recognizing all of the members who volunteer in our congregation.

❏ Our congregation regularly affirms ministry in daily life and those who make the connection.

❏ We commission and install most of those who are serving in leadership positions in the congregation.

❏ Being a disciple-leader is seen as a normal expectation of all of our members, including youth.

Chapter 4

Gifted for Leadership

The council members of Graceless Lutheran Church were concerned and becoming angry. They had two vacancies on the council and no one was willing to serve. Ernest Law, council president, explained the situation. "I have tried everything to get volunteers. I called nearly two dozen people this week, and not one of them was willing to help with anything. I told them that we had some big problems to work on, and I explained that it wouldn't take much of their time. They all had excuses. Don't these people realize what our needs are around here?" The rest of the council was silent until Helen Rash, the treasurer, asked, "What about asking one of the Morgans? They haven't been to church in quite awhile. It would be a great way to get them involved again!"

Graceless Lutheran Church doesn't exist, but its frustrations are shared by real congregations. The mistakes this congregation made in trying to identify and recruit leaders are also real. Graceless Church wasn't looking for leaders or volunteers, but for warm bodies to fill empty spaces. The council was preoccupied with its own problems, and oblivious to members' gifts, resources, and motivations. Council members were looking for organizational leaders without even taking the time to speak with candidates personally. In frustration, they began to think about recruiting people who may not have the interest or qualifications to serve on the council.

Many of us have attended meetings where everyone casts about looking for key volunteers or someone pulls out the church directory and starts calling out names of potential candidates. Effective leadership identification and recruitment doesn't work that way.

> ### It all begins with gifts
>
> Identifying leaders begins with identifying the gifts, skills, and talents that are needed. After that, we begin to look for individuals with those gifts. When we find those individuals, we need to seriously and personally discuss with them their gifts and the ministry challenges facing the congregation.

Everyone is gifted

Each of us is a gift of God, and each of us is gifted by God with unique abilities, skills, and innate talents. Part of what we are is given to us at birth, a product of our genetic inheritance. Another part of our nature is received at baptism when we become children of God. A third part of our makeup comes from the things we learn and the life we live. All of these things combine to create our giftedness.

Our gifts are not the products of luck, accident, or self-creation, but come from God: "Every generous act of giving, with every perfect gift, is from above, coming down from the Father of lights" (James 1:17). Through the eyes of faith, we can see that what we call our selves is in fact our giftedness.

We are gifted for a purpose—to build up the body of Christ and its ministry in the world (1 Corinthians 12:7). This simply means that the gifts we have received are meant to be given away. Like Abraham we have been blessed to be a blessing to others (Genesis 12:2).

As we grow in our understanding of our giftedness we also grow in our willingness to use our gifts. Our giftedness grows as we give it away! A gifted singer grows in talent as she gives away her singing. A gifted actor's skill and nuance grow with each performance. The same is true for you and for every member of your congregation.

Every person is gifted in a different way. Some people are born artists, others are drawn to athletics. Some people excel in leading

> Now there are varieties of gifts, but the same Spirit; and there are varieties of services, but the same Lord; and there are varieties of activities, but it is the same God who activates all of them in everyone. To each is given the manifestation of the Spirit for the common good.
>
> —1 Corinthians 12:4-7

groups and teaching, others thrive in a learning environment. No one person has all the gifts that are needed in the church, and no one in the church is without any gifts for ministry.

Discovering gifts

Identifying and recruiting disciple-leaders doesn't begin with identifying needs. It begins with identifying the giftedness of individuals and helping them to give themselves away for the gospel.

Opportunities for helping your congregation's members discover their giftedness are limited only by your imagination. Awakening everyone to their giftedness and call to ministry will require that you use numerous settings and programs throughout the year.

A *gift discovery* tool can help individuals begin to discern their giftedness. Expand and adapt the sample interview and checklist on pages 95-97 to fit your congregation's personality.

A *new member class* is a natural place to introduce people to their giftedness. This also signals to new members the importance of sharing themselves with others.

Bible studies using 1 Corinthians, Ephesians, 1 Peter, or related themes can introduce gifts and involve participants in self-discovery.

Adult and children's Sunday school classes provide you with built-in opportunities for Bible study and gift exploration.

Baptismal instruction for adults and parents is easily adaptable to gift discoveries, as is *marriage and pre-marital counseling*.

First communion instruction provides a wonderful setting for reflecting on Jesus' gift of himself for us and the ways in which we too might share. This is an occasion where children and parents can share their gift discoveries with each other.

Worship brings your whole congregation together, and through sermons, temple talks, liturgies, and litanies everyone can be invited to look deeper at how they have been blessed and how they might be a greater blessing to others.

Why not introduce and use a gift discovery tool during the annual *stewardship emphasis*? Many congregations have used a time and talent sheet to emphasize stewardship. The intent is good, but the follow-through is often weak and even self-defeating. However, using a gift discovery tool or interview during the annual stewardship emphasis can point out the personal blessings each member has received. Be careful, though, not to link the discoveries to "slots that need to be filled." Cottage meetings, Consecration Sundays, and even stewardship relay methods can be easily adapted to include gift discoveries.

Use *existing committees and small groups* whenever possible. If these groups have a built-in relational dynamic, then the discoveries can be made and affirmed by the whole group. If you offer *small-group and committee leadership training*, make gift identification a key element of the curriculum.

Youth ministry groups and *confirmation classes* are ideal settings for identifying gifts and celebrating the discoveries that are made. This can be helpful for youth who are looking for affirmation or direction in their lives. If your young people have retreats or lock-ins, these special events can add emphasis and depth to the discussions and discoveries.

Appreciative Inquiry (see chapter 3) provides a superb process for individual and group gift discovery. Develop your own interview protocol or use the questions in the "Appreciative Inquiry Interview Guide" on pages 89-91. Sometimes it's easier to get members talking about other people's gifts rather than their own. If this is the case in your congregation, then structure your AI questions to elicit affirmations about others.

A *congregational gift inventory* can accomplish much the same thing. (See the "Congregational Gift Inventory" tool on pages 98-99.) If you have the space, put up a congregational *gifts mural* where members are invited to write down all of the congregation's blessings. Separate the mural into sections for people, facilities, groups, programs, and so on. Members who have had difficulty seeing their own giftedness will warm to the subject as they affirm others.

Why not try *e-mail*? Send out a gift discovery interview and checklist and ask individuals to fill it out and send it back. Use e-mail to involve those members who haven't been reached by any other method. Prepare to be surprised. The response may not be great, but it will probably be better than a *church newsletter insert*.

Personalizing the process

It makes little difference whether you use existing systems, or create your own gift discovery events. However, your effectiveness will be greatly reduced if the process you use is not personalized. No system is more effective than a personal *one-on-one interview*. If all of your efforts are focused on group settings, be sure to provide for follow-up conversations with each participant. Follow-up on the discoveries that are made as soon as possible.

> **No system is more effective than a personal one-on-one interview.**

Ask yourself and those you are interviewing, "Where is God calling you to use your gifts and talents?" Don't delay in asking this! Allowing people's insights, enthusiasm, and vision to languish will not benefit them, the church, or the ministries that are waiting to happen.

Giftedness guides ministry

You have a host of programs and ministries, but after a gift discovery emphasis it may seem like you don't have the right people for the right jobs. Although your congregation is incredibly gifted, it may

Your long-term goal is to reach as many of your members as possible, and involve those who have not experienced the joy of gift discovery. It's exciting to watch and listen to people who have just begun to see themselves as gifted by God. They are like children unwrapping their presents on Christmas morning—they are surprised, excited, and anxious to show off their new possessions.

look like the members have all the wrong gifts! Before you despair, look again.

Maybe there are some individuals who are willing to stretch their skills and to receive training for new tasks and programs. In chapter 7 we'll look at some ways to help you train and retool your leaders for change. If training isn't the answer, it is probably time to let members' gifts guide the ministry of your congregation. Congregations, as you know, have great difficulty changing the way they do things. Programs, priorities, and ministries that were once vital and effective sometimes can become stale and ineffective. No one wants to admit this publicly, for fear of hurting someone's feelings. Yet, everyone may be frustrated as they continue to fail at identifying willing volunteers for certain programs.

There are at least two ways to address this situation. First, consider transforming your existing programs. Reshaping old structures will enable you to reach across generational boundaries, and appeal to new temperaments and motivations. If no one wants to serve on the kitchen crew, maybe there is something unappealing in the name as well as the job. Suggest renaming it the "Congregation Cuisine Club." Offer classes in the culinary arts, and transform church dinners into dining experiences in which volunteers show off their newly acquired skills. Women's and men's organizations are frequently frustrated by dwindling numbers and few new recruits. What would happen if those organizations gave permission for others to start small-group ministries to reach out to young parents, singles, and other new people? The program names may change, but their ministries may continue to grow.

A second way to deal with few willing volunteers for your programs is to let the giftedness of members guide the ministry of the congregation. This may mean that some of your congregation's programs and ministries are no longer relevant. It also may mean that God has gifted your congregation in new ways to enable you to move in new directions. If this seems to be the case, you may want to read one of the other books in this series, *Our Mission: Discovering God's Call to Us.*

Imagine what it would be like if your congregation were a new mission church with no organizational structure, programs, or outreach ministry. Would you begin by transplanting another congregation's structure and programs into your congregation? Or would you take the time to see how God has gifted your congregation, and begin to build on God's blessings? One of the exciting things about the gift discovery process is discovering where God is calling your congregation. When you look at how God has gifted your congregation's members, you begin to see where God is calling you to go. For instance, if you discover that you have numerous gifted teachers in your congregation, maybe it's time to begin an after school program, a day school, or an adult continuing education center. A group of people with skills in home building and repairs could mean the beginning of a Habitat for Humanity project in your community. The possibilities are as endless as the gifts God has given. When our giftedness guides the ministry we need to be prepared to go into places we have never gone before, and once again be ready to be surprised by where the Holy Spirit leads.

In this process you will also discover that God has gifted all of us for ministry in daily life. Each of us is an ambassador for Christ and his church in the world, every day of the week. As the church, we need to affirm and support those ministries that take place outside of our walls.

For more on this topic, see *Our Mission: Discovering God's Call to Us.*

God has gifted all of us for ministry in daily life.

A gift of music

Brooke joined a congregation and was baptized when she was in seventh grade. Her parents didn't participate. She joined with her friends, all of whom were invited to church by the pastor's children. The little congregation welcomed them, but had no programs to offer young people other than Sunday school. Brooke was drawn to music and singing, but the congregation's choir members were all older people and the music selections didn't sound very inviting to a 12-year-old.

One of the Sunday school teachers recognized Brooke's desire and gifts, and arranged for her to sing a contemporary gospel solo accompanied by a "boom box" one Sunday. It was the first of many musical offerings.

When Brooke's congregation let her gifts guide the ministry, everyone was blessed. Today Brooke attends a university where she is studying music. She is also playing the organ and directing the choir in a congregation very much like the one in which she was baptized.

Checklist

❑ Our congregation is helping all members discover their giftedness and callings.

❑ We let the giftedness of our members guide our ministry directions.

❑ We take the time to interview potential volunteers and discuss their giftedness with them.

❑ We prefer leaving positions vacant rather than filling slots with unqualified or uninterested individuals.

Chapter 5

Leadership Styles and Motivations

Now as they went on their way, he entered a certain village, where a woman named Martha welcomed him into her home. She had a sister named Mary, who sat at the Lord's feet and listened to what he was saying. But Martha was distracted by her many tasks; so she came to him and asked, "Lord, do you not care that my sister has left me to do all the work by myself? Tell her then to help me." But the Lord answered her, "Martha, Martha, you are worried and distracted by many things; there is need of only one thing. Mary has chosen the better part, which will not be taken away from her."

—Luke 10:38-42

The lesson of this story is quite straightforward, and hinges on Jesus' concluding comments. Mary understood what was important in life, and Martha was too concerned about worldly things. Jesus wants us to get our priorities in order. This story is also a great illustration of clashing motivations. Martha is motivated by her tasks and Mary is preoccupied with her relationships.

Recognizing and understanding our differences

Some people are similar to Martha and me. We are very focused on getting our tasks done, and done well. Others, like Mary, are preoccupied with relationships. Neither type is superior to the other, but when these two types interact without knowing their differences, friction and frustration can emerge.

This phenomena has important implications for leadership development, particularly when identifying leaders and matching them with ministries. Every existing and potential leader is a highly

The Easter breakfast

My wife and I love to prepare and serve dinners at our church. The Easter breakfast is especially rewarding for us. It's the most important day in the church year calendar, and that early morning meal is a special time of fellowship and celebration. However, for a time it was also one of the most irritating days in my calendar.

While we were frantically running around preparing the food, setting the tables, and putting on the final touches, other people would enter the kitchen and want to talk—about everything except the emerging meal. It drove me nuts! I had work to do and they wanted to discuss their child's latest exploits. I was up to my ears in scrambled eggs and pancake batter, and they were asking about the health of my parents. I thought these people were insensitive, rude, unthinking, selfish, and lazy. Why didn't they grab a dishtowel and do something?

This situation repeated itself every year, until I began to understand the motivations and needs of my kitchen visitors. Everyone wasn't just like me. In fact, no one was just like me.

complex gifted person with motivations, emotions, traits, dispositions, and needs. We need to pay careful attention to each person's uniqueness. Some individuals love parties, others prefer solitude. Group projects inspire some and frighten others. What we do, how we do it, and when we get the job done is different for everyone. Ignoring or failing to understand these differences hobbles a congregation's efforts and effectiveness in ministry.

Contemporary culture offers a wide variety of ways to categorize people: left-handed or right-handed, type A or B, birth order, left brain or right brain, and a host of other "types." The following theories have stood the test of time, and have proven to be helpful to congregations as they seek to understand individual differences and motivations.

Maslow's Hierarchy of Needs

Psychologist Abraham Maslow developed one of the most long-lived theories of motivation. Maslow observed that individuals are motivated by unmet needs, and he proposed a hierarchy of needs (see illustration). Individuals tend toward growth and love, but are unable to achieve those and other higher needs until more basic needs are met. Life, at its best, becomes an ascending journey from the lowest level on the hierarchy of needs to the top.

The most basic or *physiological needs* must be met before humans can begin to thrive in any significant way. Food, oxygen, sleep, avoidance of pain, and other primary issues must be dealt with before people can aspire to higher goals. After meeting basic human requirements, people then need to meet *safety needs*, seeking out security, stability, and protection. When safety needs predominate, humans seek out greater order and structure in their lives.

Once physiological and safety needs are met, humans are able to seek out relationships and community. The third level in the hierarchy is comprised of *belonging needs*. People express these needs in the desires to develop friendships, marry, join organizations, or create families. It is at this level that love is expressed.

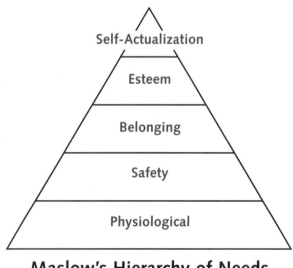

Maslow's Hierarchy of Needs

When belonging has begun to mature, humans seek to attain *esteem needs*. Esteem needs include both self-respect and the respect of others. Achievement, attention, personal mastery, confidence, independence, and freedom each describe an esteem attribute.

Only by meeting the lower needs in the hierarchy are humans able to move toward the top level, *self-actualization*. Self-actualization is the desire to reach your potential, and to be all you can be. According to Maslow, very few people ever reach this level. Among the self-actualized are Albert Einstein, Mahatma Gandhi, Eleanor Roosevelt, and Abraham Lincoln.

Implications for congregations

Anyone who has worked in a mission field or in the inner city knows that it is nearly impossible to discuss issues of faith with individuals who have no food, shelter, or other basic necessities of life. The same is true of safety needs. If people do not feel secure or protected, it is extremely difficult to engage them in relationships and community.

This same dynamic is true in your congregation. If members are having difficulty meeting their basic needs, they will be unwilling and unable to participate in community-building activities. Similarly, if your members feel insecure or unsafe in your congregation's neighborhood, no amount of cajoling will get them involved.

Many inner city congregations face these obstacles every day. Yet, some are flourishing, with many of the neighborhood residents actively involved in the church's ministries and leadership. In general, these congregations are active throughout the week providing food, employment, and social services for their neighbors. Car pooling and parking lot monitors help maintain a safe environment. Because these congregations help people meet their physiological and safety needs, they are able to provide ministries that offer a sense of belonging and growth in self-esteem.

Maslow's
theories
highlight the
importance of
recognizing
people's needs,
and meeting
people where
they are.

Maslow's theories highlight the importance of recognizing people's needs, and meeting people where they are. Inviting people to participate and lead at levels of the hierarchy beyond their present level is fruitless unless you are able and willing to provide for their more fundamental needs. In short, offering community, self-esteem, and self-actualization before basic needs are met is usually a waste of time. Likewise, efforts to recruit individuals to participate and lead in ministries that focus beyond their present unmet needs will fail.

Maslow believed that his hierarchy of needs could also apply to organizations and institutions. Where does your congregation fit in the hierarchy of needs? You may want to adapt your ministries and programs to meet unmet corporate needs and invite members of your congregation to explore the next level of the hierarchy.

McClelland's theory of motivation

Another perspective on motivation was developed by David McClelland and John Atkinson. This theory suggests that there are three types of motivation: achievement, affiliation, and power. According to McClelland, each person is motivated primarily by one of these types. Take the "Motivation Self-Test" on page 100 to identify your motivation type.

Achievers love to solve problems. These are the individuals who like to take on thorny issues and problems that arise in an organization. They are concerned with setting personal goals and attaining them while overcoming the obstacles that get in the way. They like to work alone and will bend the rules to get the job done. Achievers think about accomplishing important things and advancing their careers. Achievers seek out specific feedback from others—they want to know if they are getting the job done, and getting it done better, quicker, and more creatively.

Affiliators are very different from achievers. They are motivated by relationships and interpersonal interaction. These are the "people persons" in an organization. Affiliators place great importance on being liked by others and in maintaining harmony and cohesion in groups. Affiliators will frequently avoid conflict. They are the caregivers, the sympathetic ears, and the shoulders to cry on in an organization.

Power-motivated people are most concerned about influencing others. These individuals have a strong desire to change other people's behavior and ideas. Power people are often very verbal, outspoken, and forceful. Power people are often seen as leaders—winning arguments, directing others, beating the competition, and growing in status. This motivating force, as you might expect, comes in both positive (socialized) and negative (personalized) types. In the positive type, people exercise their power and influence on behalf of others, creating shared ownership by their leadership. In the negative type, people are concerned with their own personal dominance, prestige, and authority.

Implications for congregations

McClelland's theory is extremely helpful for congregations as they match their members with specific jobs and ministries. Knowing your primary motivation and the motivations of others can also be invaluable in understanding group dynamics, conflict, and change.

Affiliators are the people that you want as greeters, callers, and fellowship planners. These are the individuals that create the "glue" in a community. Affiliators provide the relational dimension in small groups and committees. They are the home visitors, hosts, counselors, party animals, and listeners. Affiliators can also drive people motivated by achievement or power crazy! They will want to constantly talk, share, and discuss things (like dinner decorations or family issues) that your more goal-oriented people may find unnecessary or unhelpful for the job at hand.

Members who are achievers are best suited to developing new programs, strategies, objectives, and visions. They grow bored providing ongoing maintenance for programs and activities. Achievers love to analyze the situation and develop strategies for getting the job done. Achievers do well on serving on task forces, planning and running campaigns, and setting a vision for the congregation. Affiliators are baffled by achievers, and sometimes irritated because they don't seem to be relaxed or enjoying the people around them.

The people motivated by power in your congregation are the ones who like to make things happen. They enjoy developing policies, raising money, dealing with other power brokers, and making sure the congregation is doing what it should be doing. These people are excited when they are able to teach, preach, lead, or otherwise influence the direction and future of the congregation. A gifted power person can inspire the entire congregation and help it to reach its potential.

McClelland's theory reminds us that everyone is not concerned or excited about the same things in the congregation or in life. The ideas and projects that enliven and animate one person are sometimes of little interest to another. It may be helpful to incorporate McClelland's theory in your gift discovery process, new member classes, and leadership training events.

The Myers-Briggs Type Indicator

The Myers-Briggs Type Indicator (MBTI) was developed in the early 1940s as a tool for helping individuals identify their psychological types. The MBTI is widely used in business, education, and government to identify individuals' preferences, interests, needs, and motivations. One to two million people take the MBTI every year.

The MBTI measures your tendency toward the following:
1. introversion or extraversion (E-I)
2. sensing or intuition (S-N)
3. thinking or feeling (T-F)
4. judging or perceiving (J-P)

Results of the test are given in a group of four letters that describe your present type, such as INTJ (introvert, intuitive, thinking, judging).

Implications for congregations

Many congregations have found that using the MBTI has been very helpful, particularly when used by the staff, the leadership team, or the council. Consider using the MBTI in any serious leadership development, community building, or gifts discovery effort.

A full description of the MBTI and the 16 different types is not possible in this book, but you can get a basic idea about your type by filling out the "Personal Preferences" tool on pages 101-103. For a thorough individual or group typing, contact a trained MBTI counselor in your area. *God's Gifted People: Discovering Your Personality as a Gift* by Gary Harbaugh (Minneapolis: Augsburg, 1990, ISBN 0-8066-2486-8), can help explain and apply the MBTI to your congregation and your God-given gifts.

Reprise

If only we had known! Martha was obviously an achiever with some self-esteem issues to deal with. Mary, the affiliator, was driving Martha crazy and probably didn't even know it. Was Mary working through some belonging needs, or was she heading toward self-actualization? If only we had seen their MBTIs!

Psychological theories and testing really add nothing to the story of Martha and Mary, but they do add to our understandings about one another, and how different we are in our giftedness. Each of us is wonderfully different than everyone else. We are the products of God's grace, our own unique environments, and our genetic predispositions. Understanding the gift of diversity and the individual preferences and motivations in your congregation will help you immeasurably as you seek to identify, recruit, support, and evaluate potential leaders.

Each of us is wonderfully different than everyone else.

Checklist

❏ Our congregation makes an intentional effort to understand individual preferences and motivations when recruiting volunteers.

❏ Our council and committees regularly discuss individual preferences and leadership styles and how they impact group effectiveness.

❏ A major part of our leadership training involves reflection on individual differences in style, preference, and motivation.

❏ Our congregation uses a gift discovery process that includes elements related to personal preferences and motivation.

❏ We have discussed where our congregation is located on Maslow's hierarchy of needs, and have begun to adapt and develop our ministry to reflect our findings.

Chapter 6

Recruiting Leaders

From that time Jesus began to proclaim, "Repent, for the kingdom of heaven has come near."

As he walked by the Sea of Galilee, he saw two brothers, Simon, who is called Peter, and Andrew his brother, casting a net into the sea—for they were fishermen. And he said to them, "Follow me, and I will make you fish for people." Immediately they left their nets and followed him.

—Matthew 4:17-20

That is perhaps the quickest and most effective leadership recruitment story in the Bible. A brief invitation is given to two busy fishermen, and without discussion they follow this man called Jesus. Why was Jesus so successful? Why can't you and I experience those same kinds of results when we invite others to volunteer?

Elements of effective invitations

In spite of the brevity of the story, Matthew has described the four essential elements of effective recruitment invitations:

1. a vision of the ministry
2. an appreciation of giftedness
3. a description of the ministry task
4. a declaration of the impact that the volunteers can make in the ministry

This chapter explores these four components of invitations. Without these elements, we are only filling slots. We'll also look at practical guidelines for recruitment.

Providing a vision of the ministry

A vision is a picture of a preferred future. With a vision, congregations know where they want to go and what they want to accomplish. Without a vision congregations are lost, wandering in countless directions, following the whims of the day, and spending their energy reacting to the moment's issues, pressures, and problems. A vision gives the congregation's ministry coherence. It helps make sense of all the programs, ministries, tasks, and events that fill the calendar.

A vision gives the congregation's ministry coherence.

At its best a vision is faithful. A well-articulated vision answers the question, what is God's purpose for this congregation? When a vision is not clear or faithful, people are reticent to come forward and participate in the life of the parish. In Matthew's text, Jesus has proclaimed the vision: "Repent, for the kingdom of heaven has come near." That's the big picture that drew Peter and Andrew away from their nets and toward Jesus. If they had known nothing about Jesus' preaching and vision, it is highly unlikely that they would have so readily followed him.

As you begin to recruit and invite others to participate in the ministry of your congregation, make sure that you can articulate the big picture. Your statement of vision should answer many of the following questions for potential leaders and volunteers:

- What is the faithful thing to do?
- Why are we doing this?
- Why is this important?
- What does this have to do with me?
- What do you want to accomplish?
- Where do I fit in?
- Is this something worth doing?

Peter and Andrew might not have asked all those questions, but they certainly thought about some of them. Jesus' vision and proclamation about the kingdom made it clear to them where Jesus was leading and why. Jesus' vision was compelling and exciting. It was a big vision that captured their imagination and made it possible for them to set aside what they were doing.

Is your congregation's vision faithful and compelling? Are members of your congregation excited about God's future for them? If the answer is yes, that's great. If the answer is no, then take the time now to discern and articulate a preferred future.

Begin all of your recruitment invitations, whether on the phone or in person, with a brief description of the bigger vision, purpose, or mission of the congregation. "Bob, you know how First Church is really committed to serving the new growing immigrant population in our community; that's why we need your help." Beginning your inquiry in this way serves two purposes. It sets your conversation in a wider context that makes clear the congregation's priorities and invites Bob's active participation. Bob now knows where he fits in the bigger picture, and he knows that he isn't just filling a slot.

You may find that Bob does not like the congregation's vision for ministry. If that is the case, it is better that you find that out up front, and not risk jeopardizing the vision with half-hearted volunteers.

*For assistance in this task, see **Our Mission: Discovering God's Call to Us.***

Appreciating giftedness

When Jesus called Peter and Andrew he invited them to use their gifts and skills. He invited them to a new ministry, but they could keep on fishing. Jesus appreciated the skills and gifts that they had acquired; he didn't try to put round pegs in square holes. He didn't say, "Follow me and I will make you carpenters of people." His invitation recognized the gifts of those being invited.

The same should be true of our efforts. In chapters 4 and 5 we discussed both the gifts and the motivations of the members of your congregation. It is imperative that this information not be forgotten. All of our recruitment efforts should be permeated with an appreciation of each individual's gifts, skills, talents, and traits. Additionally we need to be sensitive to each individual's availability. Not all people are able to make long-term commitments, or to volunteer during the day,

When Jesus called Peter and Andrew he invited them to use their gifts and skills.

or to find babysitters to watch their children. Time is also a gift, and everyone is gifted in different ways. Each of us has experienced the frustration of trying to accomplish a task that was a mismatch for us. Those mismatches probably caused us frustration and undoubtedly also frustrated the people who asked us to do the jobs. Simply filling slots while disregarding individual gifts, motivations, and availability will accomplish neither long-range nor short-range goals.

Describing the ministry task

The third component of effective leadership recruitment is providing ministry descriptions. Potential volunteers and leaders want to know what is expected of them. No one wants to fail at a task. Ministry descriptions, even brief ones, can help people quickly recognize whether they are gifted for or able to accomplish a given task. Ministry descriptions also help you avoid misunderstandings about expectations, supervision, accountabilities, responsibilities, and closure.

No ministry is too small or unimportant to require a ministry description. Potential greeters want to know where they should stand and what they should say. Kitchen helpers want to know who is in

---

An effective ministry description includes the following elements:
- Position title (such as nursery attendant)
- Basic responsibilities
- The amount of time involved (for example, 4 hours a month)
- The timeline involved
- The goals to be accomplished
- Who is supervising this position
- What training and support will be provided
- How and when the work will be evaluated

charge, and where to find the can openers. Office volunteers want to know how long it takes to fold and staple the monthly newsletter. Every job has unique elements, but we can't assume that everyone knows what those are. Use the "Ministry Description Form" on pages 104-105, or create a form of your own, to provide information about each ministry in your congregation.

Once you have developed a ministry description, invite volunteers to provide feedback regarding the description's accuracy and helpfulness. Review and update your ministry descriptions annually. One congregation had a ministry description for the custodian that was 30 years old. The custodian diligently and thoroughly accomplished everything on this list of duties. Yet, everyone complained about the custodian's work. The ministry description (and the salary) hadn't changed but the building, the congregation, and the programs had doubled in size.

Review and update your ministry descriptions annually.

Making a difference

Every potential volunteer and leader wants to know how their efforts are making a difference—a difference for the gospel, for other people, and for the world. When inviting and recruiting others it is critical to make the connection between the proposed position and its impact on the vision and ministry of the congregation. Why is painting the Sunday school rooms important? What difference does it make if we have a nursery attendant? Why do we need this particular committee?

Don't inflate or deflate the importance of various ministries. Either way, you distort everyone's expectations. Keep your description of the ministry's impact simple and straightforward, and relate it to the wider ministry of the congregation: "Helen, your help as a nursery attendant will enable us to reach out much more effectively to new young families. These families expect a well-staffed, modern nursery, and you can help us make that happen."

Busy work is seldom if ever rewarding to the volunteer or the congregation. Explaining the ministry impact of various jobs to potential volunteers has the added benefit of helping you understand the value of the jobs and the volunteers. If you are recruiting people for jobs that have little or no meaning, end the recruiting or end the jobs.

Recruitment guidelines

A one-on-one interview is almost always the most effective way of inviting someone to serve. Taking the time to discuss gifts, challenges, and ministry descriptions is time well spent. A good rule of thumb suggests that the more important the task, the more important the interview. A telephone interview to a prospective candidate is appropriate if the volunteer activity is relatively simple or if the task requires only a short-term commitment. Identifying and recruiting nominees for the church council or the long-range planning committee require in-depth discussion. Finding someone to fold bulletins for an afternoon does not.

The more important the task, the more important the interview.

Do not make blanket requests for volunteers when you are seeking to fill important positions. One congregation made the mistake of putting this announcement in its Sunday bulletin: "Anyone wishing to serve on the congregation council should see Gloria after worship." That announcement attracted several people known as troublemakers who were very excited about being on the council, and sharing their gripes monthly. The problem was then compounded when these volunteers were not nominated for the council positions.

When you are recruiting, let people say no. Trying to force people to serve, through guilt or other means, accomplishes nothing. Take no for an answer, and use this opportunity to find out how and when this person would like to serve in the future. Very often, you will be surprised by the ministries in which members would like to participate. If the "no" answer is related to timing, ask about the person's future availability, and take note of opportunities for future service. Keep the door open for later involvement.

Coordinating recruitment

Inviting others to serve is a critical task, and not everyone is gifted at it. If your committee chairpersons are expected to do recruiting, then provide them with the tools and training they need to be effective.

The leadership identification and recruitment task should be dispersed throughout the congregation. Very often congregations rely on the pastor or the council president to do the majority of the recruiting. These individuals should be used as recruiters, but only for the most important or challenging positions in the congregation. The Worship Committee can identify greeters, ushers, and worship assistants. The Property Committee can identify people to mow the lawn, weed the flower beds, and so on. Sharing the recruitment task demonstrates the communal nature of the congregation's life and ministry.

A nominating committee, congregation council, church staff, or ministry coordinator (volunteer or paid position) may provide coordination so that the same person is not recruited for several tasks at the same time. The book *Our Staff: Building Our Human Resources* can help you decide whether a staff position is needed for this coordination of efforts.

The leadership identification and recruitment task should be dispersed throughout the congregation.

See *Our Staff: Building Our Human Resources.*

We were afraid of goofing up!

Every congregation has tasks and ministries that seem easy to do, if you are an insider. If you are new or uninitiated, those same tasks appear to be comprised of secret handshakes and other arcane knowledge. That was the situation when First Church was desperately looking for people to be ushers. First Church was a small congregation. The same people were ushering every week, and they were tired.

The situation changed when the pastor and congregation council planned and implemented a training event for ushers, greeters, and worship leaders. Potential volunteers were promised a ministry description and an opportunity to walk through their worship responsibilities. Developing the ministry descriptions also provided the pastor and Worship Committee with an opportunity to make some needed changes in the worship environment.

The results were very surprising. A dozen new people volunteered, and the longtime volunteers were given a break. More importantly, once the mystery was taken out of some of the volunteer positions, new members as well as longtime members who had always been a little intimidated by the jobs were now glad to serve.

Katherine, who had been a member of First Church for 40 years, spoke for most of the new volunteers when she said, "I didn't know what the ushers were supposed to do, so I was always afraid to say I'd volunteer. I thought that if I did volunteer, I'd probably goof up and offend someone."

The new volunteers didn't goof up, the mystery was removed from several ministries, and the worship practices of First Church were updated and improved.

Checklist

❑ We know who is responsible for recruiting people for the various ministry positions in our congregation.

❑ We have developed and updated most of the ministry and job descriptions in our congregation.

❑ Our congregation has a clearly articulated vision or purpose statement.

❑ Leaders and volunteers understand how their efforts fit into the wider ministry of the congregation.

❑ Every effort is made to match an individual's gifts with specific ministry needs.

❑ We have identified a specific group or person to coordinate our recruitment efforts.

Chapter 7

Developing Leaders

So neither the one who plants nor the one who waters is anything,
but only God who gives the growth.

—1 Corinthians 3:7

How do we grow more disciple-leaders? We don't! Only God gives
the growth. Leaders and volunteers are gifts given to us by God. They
are, as in Paul's analogy, like seeds that we plant in our garden. We
don't make the seeds, and we can't create the life and the growth in
those seeds. But we can take what God has given us and tend it like
faithful gardeners. Disciple-leaders are already in your congregation.
The seeds have been planted. Your task and mine is to water them,
fertilize them, prune them, and nurture them in ways that will help
them sprout and grow. You may want to think of this chapter as a gardener's guide to leadership development.

Five ways to nurture leadership development

St. Peter's Church didn't start out by developing a comprehensive
plan for leadership training and support, but that's what happened.
When they initiated a comprehensive small-group ministry, they
incorporated a wide variety of learning and development styles that
met the diverse needs of the congregation's disciple-leaders.

Disciple-leaders at St. Peter's were developed in at least five different ways:

1. Experience
2. Example
3. Feedback
4. Learning
5. Teaching

Leaders in training

St. Peter's Church wanted to grow, and its leaders were anxious to renew the life of the parish. Pastor Chris and the congregation council wanted to reach out to the neighborhood and invite people in. They also knew that they had to make a concerted effort to identify and develop new disciple-leaders in the congregation. Their renewal effort began with the development of a comprehensive small-group ministry.

Pastor Chris and the council began by identifying and recruiting a dozen potential small-group leaders. These people were invited to a training event that consisted of lectures, discussion, role playing, and skill practice. After the initial training, small groups were formed. Each group had a group leader and an apprentice leader. The small-group ministry coordinator provided regular feedback and evaluation for each of the leaders and the apprentices. The apprentices practiced leading as the small groups grew. They became group leaders when the groups divided and multiplied.

Renewal in the church's life and growth in numbers began and continued. Small-group members were nourished in the faith, and leaders were shaped by a comprehensive support system. Several years later Pastor Chris was asked to explain his congregation's growth to a churchwide representative. Without hesitation he responded, "Our small-group ministry—we got everyone involved, even the teenagers, and we grew leaders."

Using all or most of these methods can help you ensure effective leadership development in your congregation.

1. Experience

As a child, whenever I was hesitant about trying some new venture, my mother would say, "The only way you will find out is if you try!" Her advice was usually good, and I would attempt the new task. Developing leaders usually begins by getting someone to try something that they haven't done before. At St. Peter's, potential small-group leaders were given an orientation and then an opportunity to practice leading a small group. The small group, comprised of other potential leaders, was a comfortable and relaxed place to experience leadership. Using role-plays during training or orientation events gives new leaders a nonthreatening way to experience a new task or environment. Often that experience is enough to convince someone that they can accomplish something that they didn't think they were capable of doing. This type of training also allows the participants the opportunity to fail and try again.

2. Example

St. Peter's small-group ministry program had a built in apprenticeship. Individuals who were not ready to lead a group could watch someone else lead, spread their wings when they were ready, and discuss their progress with a mentor. This form of leadership development is very similar to Jesus' commission to the 70 (Luke 10:1), when he sent his disciples out in pairs for mutual support and encouragement.

Partnering emerging leaders with experienced ones creates a training environment that also ensures that the task will be done correctly. This type of training has the added benefit of improving the performance and intentionality of existing leaders. After all, if you are asked to be a mentor you are usually honored to be asked and want to do your very best!

3. Feedback

Feedback is closely related to learning by example or mentoring. New disciple-leaders want to succeed at their ministries, and constant affirmative evaluation and coaching can help make that happen. The keys to successful feedback are immediacy and positive reinforcement. Negative feedback delivered long after the fact creates unhealthy relationships and very frustrated volunteers and leaders.

My grandfather was my mentor and coach through much of my childhood, and his great gift was patient, positive feedback. As he taught me how to work with wood, his comments were few but unfailingly helpful. "Are you sure you want to cut that board there? Try measuring one more time and see what happens." When a project was done, he always complimented me on the work, and asked me what I could have done differently. I usually knew what needed improvement, and his positive comments encouraged me to improve and excel.

4. Learning

Learning means being exposed to new ideas and information, and that can happen in a wide variety of ways and settings. When we think of learning we usually visualize a classroom. At St. Peter's the classroom for leadership development was provided during the initial orientation and small-group leader workshop. Other in-service opportunities were provided as the program matured.

Workshops, classes, retreats, and orientations are necessary for presenting new information to a group of people. However, their effectiveness is limited if the participants are not able to immediately act upon the information they receive. Creating effective learning events means that you will also have to provide hands-on experiences. At St. Peter's, role-plays strengthened the learning provided in workshops. Immediately after the workshop small groups were formed and began functioning. When you plan learning events, be sure to include a

Creating effective learning events means that you will also have to provide hands-on experiences.

goal-setting segment, some experiential learning, a summary of the main points, and immediate follow-up steps.

5. Teaching

One of the best ways to learn is to teach. Sharing information and new ideas with others requires both discipline and organization. I have often been called upon to present material that I have not fully mastered. Teaching in these situations caused me to take time to study, reflect on, and organize the material. Teaching helps the learner/teacher to crystallize thoughts and assimilate new information. Is there someone on your congregation council who could run a workshop on effective meetings? Is there a Sunday school teacher who could teach others about how we learn? Are there people in your congregation who have never taught anything, but who have information of value for everyone? Giving these people the opportunity to teach others will help them to mature in their skills, while providing new information and learning opportunities for others.

Your leadership development plan

Some congregations provide occasional leadership training events, but most provide little or no ongoing leadership training and development. Effective congregations have a leadership development plan that is implemented year-round and adjusted to meet changing needs. Before you begin offering leadership events, workshops, and retreats, take the time to develop a year-round plan. You or your planning group should be able to answer the following questions:

Effective congregations have a leadership development plan.

- What training has been provided in the past? Was it effective? Was it well received?

- What individuals and groups do you want to impact immediately? Later?

- How many members do you want to involve in the coming year?

- What leadership skills and training are needed?

- What leadership skills need improvement?

- How will your development plan support and strengthen the congregation's mission and vision?

When you have answered those and other questions, set up a timeline for your various events.

Orientation and training for the congregation council

Leadership development and training for the congregation council is usually most helpful at the beginning of the year, or whenever a new council is elected. The agenda for that training can include a wide variety of orientation information:

- how to run a meeting
- how the congregation is structured
- how to set an agenda
- the congregation's mission and vision

Orientation and training for other groups

This annual orientation and training event for new council members and existing leaders should set the tone for the coming year, and also provide a model for all other congregational leadership development events. An all-day event or overnight retreat is preferable to a workshop or mini-training event, but do what works best in your congregation. See the "Sample Agenda for a Leadership Retreat" on pages 106-108.

Other congregational training events can be offered in locations and times limited only by your imagination. Include leadership training and development in Saturday workshops, lay schools of theology, Sunday school classes, annual meetings, meetings after Sunday worship services, new member classes, Lenten and Advent midweek events, a sermon series, and so on.

Four factors to consider in your plan

The quality of the content, styles of training, motivations of your participants, and the locations and accommodations for events are all critical considerations in your planning for leadership development.

Quality

When we provide mundane leadership training that applies only to our congregation, we fail to inspire the participants and we fail to build leaders. The training that we provide should be superior in content and presentation, and the skills that we teach should be transferrable to people's daily lives. St. Peter's small-group ministry training focused on Bible study, prayer, and faith sharing. Participants received excellent information related to group dynamics, active listening, conflict resolution, and much more.

Learning styles

Training experiences should also incorporate a variety of learning styles in order to impact the widest possible audience. Blending discussion, lectures, experiential learning, and relationship building creates an educational smorgasbord that meets the differing needs of participants.

Motivations

Consider the motivations of your participants when planning and holding training events. Beginning and ending your events on time and including problem solving situations will endear you to your achievers. Offering fellowship and relationship building opportunities will win you the thanks of your affiliators. Providing content that promises to make an impact on participants and the wider community will be highly attractive to those who are motivated by power and influence. No single strategy will be effective with everyone. Variety is the spice of leadership development.

Location and accommodations

Don't underestimate the importance of location and accommodations when planning your leadership training events. Important training events are more effective when located away from the congregation's building. Meeting in another church building, a hotel, or retreat facility reduces distractions, and heightens the significance of the event.

Whether you meet on site or off, arrange your accommodations to reflect your training goals. A classroom setting suggests a lecture format and an individual learning environment. Chairs placed around a table produce a group task-oriented environment. Easy chairs arranged in a comfortable lounge space are ideal for community and relationship building. During retreats and all day events, change the type of setting several times. Moving from a lounge area to a conference table (or vice versa) is a great way to signal a change in direction for the participants and the agenda. Changing your setting also enhances your ability to address the varying motivations of your participants.

Arrange your accommodations to reflect your training goals.

In short, when planning your leadership training events, know your development objectives, seek to provide excellence in content and process, and provide a variety of styles and settings to meet your members' needs and motivations. Like a master gardener, plan carefully, prepare the soil, plant tenderly, water generously, and provide the right fertilizer for each plant. God will give the growth.

Checklist

❑ Our congregation provides an annual orientation and training event for the congregation council.

❑ Our congregation has an annual leadership development plan.

❑ We frequently use other locations for our training events.

❑ Our leadership development events are firmly grounded in Word and Sacrament.

❑ Our training events appeal to members with differing needs and motivations.

❑ We regularly use the following training styles:

_____ experience

_____ example

_____ feedback

_____ learning

_____ teaching

Chapter 8

Conclusion

A disciple-leader is someone who is called by God and the church to grow in his or her faith and to courageously and joyfully share that faith with others through word and action.

That is the definition of a disciple-leader. It is also a description of your calling and mine. When you and I look in a mirror we may not see a disciple-leader, but God does! We can plant, we can water, we can prune, but God gives the growth. Our calling as disciple-leaders and our efforts to develop other leaders are both gifts of God. Keep this in mind as you implement your congregation's plans for identifying and developing leaders.

We are called to be patient and expectant in our efforts. We are called to be trusting and hopeful in our planning, and we can faithfully respond to that calling because we know that all of our efforts are in God's hands. We are even free to fail, because we know that the ultimate outcome of our efforts is a gracious gift grown by God.

Called by God and the church

It is no accident that you are a Christian, and it is no mistake that you are one of Jesus' disciple-leaders. Your call to discipleship is a gift of God received in baptism. It is also no surprise that you are now looking for ways to help others grow in faith and leadership—that is part of every Christian's calling. You have been blessed to be a blessing to others: "So then, whenever we have an opportunity, let us work for the good of all, and especially for those of the family of faith" (Galatians 6:10).

The leadership development programs that you implement for your congregation are ministries. They are neither an accident of fate nor a product of luck. Whether you are a pastor or a layperson, the task of lifting up fellow Christians for service, and supporting them and strengthening them as they grow, is a high and holy calling. You are not doing this ministry simply because you were asked to do it. You have been called and gifted by God, and God will give the growth.

Growing in faith

Disciple-leaders like you and me are not born with perfect faith, and we never attain perfect faith. Our faith is never complete. Faith is always becoming something new for those who call themselves Christians. As you plan and implement programs in leadership development, recognize that you will never "arrive." Your efforts and the efforts of others represent only a piece of God's endless timeline. Building disciple-leaders has been going on for 2,000 years, and it will continue until a new age dawns.

We, as Christians, are called to be transformed and to transform the world around us: "Do not be conformed to this world, but be transformed by the renewing of your minds, so that you may discern what is the will of God—what is good and acceptable and perfect" (Romans 12:2). This is a long-term process, not a short-term program or emphasis. God will give the growth.

Don't be discouraged

God gives you courage to be a disciple-leader.

God gives you courage to be a disciple-leader—courage to speak up and to act in spite of the difficulties that may arise. As you probably know from past experience, some members of the congregation will resist new ideas, plans, and initiatives. Plans and new programs for leadership recruitment and development will undoubtedly attract detractors. Don't be discouraged but "be strong in the Lord and in the strength of his power" (Ephesians 6:10).

Keep everyone informed at all times about new initiatives. Communicate constantly with the leaders and congregation. Listen carefully and appreciatively to constructive criticism. If conflict erupts or persists, consult with your pastor or congregation council. Don't carry the burden alone!

Enjoy!

As Paul wrote in Philippians 4:4, "Rejoice in the Lord always; again I will say, Rejoice." When you plan leadership programs in your congregation, fill them with a healthy dose of joy. Ask yourself constantly: Will this event or program bring joy to those who participate? Am I having fun and finding joy in this task? Am I planning leadership ministries that are characterized by thanksgiving, blessing, and praise? If the answer to each question isn't "yes," then it's time to rethink and re-plan.

Remember, the church is not a problem to be solved, but a miracle to be appreciated. As a disciple leader, God invites you to see God's people through new eyes. The congregation, in spite of its problems and failings, is a precious and beautiful creation. It is a joy to behold.

Sharing the faith

Being a disciple-leader is not your final goal. That is only the beginning. Your goal is to help others discover their calling and grow as disciple-leaders. You and I work at this ministry for the sake of others and the world. We concern ourselves with finding and developing leaders so that we might share with them the gospel of Jesus Christ. When we identify the gifts that God has given to others, and help those people give their gifts away, the good news comes alive and God's world is changed.

See *Our Community: Dealing with Conflict in Our Congregation* for helpful ways to manage and resolve conflict.

The church is not a problem to be solved, but a miracle to be appreciated.

Closing prayer

Almighty God, we praise you for the men and women you have sent to call the Church to its tasks and renew its life. Raise up in our own day teachers and prophets inspired by your Spirit, whose voices will give strength to your Church and proclaim the reality of your kingdom; through your Son, Jesus Christ our Lord. Amen

—copyright © 1978 *Lutheran Book of Worship*

Recommended Resources

Various writers. The Congregational Leader Series. Minneapolis: Augsburg Fortress, 2002.

Boese, R. Neal. *Seven Steps and You Will Grow*. Erlanger, Ky: Seven Steps Ministries, 1994.

———. *Spiritual Gifts*. Lima, Ohio: Fairway Press, 1995.

Campbell, G. Dennis. *Congregations as Learning Communities*. The Alban Institute, 2000.

Cooperrider, David L. and Diana Whitney. *Appreciative Inquiry*. San Francisco: Berrett-Koehler Communications, Inc., 1999.

DePree, Max. *Leadership Jazz*. New York: Bantam Doubleday Dell Publishing Group, 1992.

———. *Leading Without Power*. Holland, Mich.: Shepherd Foundation, 1997.

Gilmore, Susan K., and Patrick W. Fraleigh. *Communication at Work*. Eugene, Ore.: Friendly Press, 1993.

———. *Working with Style*. Eugene, Ore: Friendly Press, 1992.

Harbaugh, Gary. *God's Gifted People: Discovering Your Personality as a Gift*. Minneapolis: Augsburg, 1990.

Hestenes, Roberta. *Turning Committees into Communities*. Colorado Springs, Colo.: NavPress, 1992.

Johnson, George S., David P. Mayer, and Nancy Vogel. *Starting Small Groups and Keeping Them Going*. Minneapolis: Augsburg Fortress, 1995.

Mann, Alice. *The In-Between Church*. The Alban Institute, 1998.

Mead, Loren B. *The Once and Future Church*. The Alban Institute, 1991.

———. *Transforming Congregations for the Future*. The Alban Institute, 1994.

Papero, Daniel V. Bowen. *Family Systems Theory*. Needham Heights, Mass.: Allyn and Bacon, 1990.

Pruyser, Paul W. *The Minister as Diagnostician.* Philadelphia: Westminster Press, 1976.

Steinke, Peter L. *Healthy Congregations.* The Alban Institute, 1996.

Trumbauer, Jean Morris. *Sharing the Ministry.* Minneapolis: Augsburg Fortress, 1995.

Watkins, Jane Magruder, and Bernard J. Mohr. *Appreciative Inquiry.* San Francisco: Jossey-Bass/Pfeiffer, 2001.

Wilson, Marlene. *The Effective Management of Volunteer Programs.* Boulder, Colo.: Volunteer Management Associates, 1976.

Chapter 1 Tool

Leadership Bible Study

Use this tool in congregation council meetings and retreats, committee meetings, adult forums, and so on.

Opening prayer

Dear Lord, thank you for blessing us with all of the gifts we need to do your work in this congregation and community. Help us to constantly acknowledge your gifts to us, and give us the generosity of spirit to give our gifts to others. Amen

Discussion starters

Choose one or more questions and invite everyone to share.

- Who was the finest leader you have ever personally known?

- What makes someone a hero? Have you ever known a hero?

- Tell a story about a boss or teacher who drove you crazy. What was it that drove you crazy?

Scripture reading

Read Acts 4:1-4, 13. The Acts of the Apostles is a chronicle of the Holy Spirit's work among the apostles. The stories and sermons that fill its pages are testimonies to the faith, struggles, and victories of the church's first leaders. These leaders and how they led are at the center of the narrative. They weren't much different from you and me.

Discussion

- What one-word description would you give for the actions of Peter and John?

- What leadership characteristics did Peter and John display?

- What leadership qualities did the priests and Sadducees demonstrate?

Going deeper

Working in pairs or small groups, read two or three of the following texts and identify the leadership qualities, traits, and skills of the characters.

Acts 1:6-8	Acts 2:1-4	Acts 2:42-47
Acts 4:32-35	Acts 6:1-8	Acts 11:19-26

In the larger group, have the small groups share the results of their discussions. List all of the leadership characteristics that were identified. Reflect together on the following questions.

- Which leadership qualities do we have in our congregation?

- Which qualities do we wish we had in our congregation?

- Where do leaders come from? What creates leadership?

Closing prayer

Thank you for all the leaders you have given the church. We give thanks especially for those who have touched and led us . . . *pause to name leaders in your lives* . . . Help each of us to grow in faith, courage, and the willingness to share your gospel in word and deed. In Christ's name we pray. Amen

Chapter 3 Tool

Appreciative Inquiry Interview Guide

Note: Adapt this interview guide as needed for use in your congregation.

Introduction

Thank you for taking the time to be interviewed. As you may know, we are hoping to interview most of our members during the next few weeks to find out what excites them about the ministries of our congregation. In these interviews we are paying particularly close attention to ways in which people are encouraged to volunteer for service, and ways in which we can support our volunteers and leaders.

All of the questions I ask will be very positive in nature. If we focused on the negatives and problems in our congregation we would only generate more negatives and problems. By focusing on the positive and the best of this congregation we hope to build from strength and expand those things that are the best of what is happening here. Before we begin, do you have any questions or concerns?

1. Tell me a story about a time when everyone in the congregation was excited, active, and involved in accomplishing something together. What happened? How did everyone get involved? Who led the effort? What made this moment special?

2. Tell me a story about a time when you felt very affirmed and appreciated by this congregation. What happened? Who was involved?

3. How has God blessed the people of this congregation? In other words, what gifts have members received for doing ministry here?

4. If you could have three wishes about volunteering, leadership, and participation in our congregation, what would they be? Don't hold back, make your wishes big ones!

5. What do you think God wants to have happen in our congregation to increase the number of people who are actively involved in the ministry here? What is God's leadership dream for our congregation?

Name of person interviewed _____

Date_____

Chapter 3 Tool

Appreciative Inquiry Planning Process

Step 1: Background and foundation

The congregation's staff and leaders begin the process by reading the background information on Appreciative Inquiry (AI) and discussing their findings with the congregation council. Following the council's approval, select an AI Steering Committee of five to eight creative and empathetic individuals. Begin informing the congregation about system-wide change and Appreciative Inquiry. Commission the Steering Committee for this ministry.

Step 2: Planning the process

First, as a Steering Committee decide on the wording for your interview guide. (Keep it very positive and inviting.) Second, decide on individual and/or group interviews. Third, interview one another individually and reflect on the quality of your interview guide and interview styles. Make any necessary changes. If you are planning individual interviews you now need to recruit an adequate number of volunteer interviewers and provide an orientation. Finally, set up a schedule for interviews, making every effort to maximize participation. You can recruit people by phone or in person, use a sign-up sheet, or allow individuals to drop in. If members are resistant, find out if it is possible to interview groups of people together at existing meetings (choir, women's groups, men's groups, and so on). Keep the congregation informed constantly.

Step 3: Interviews

Try to schedule all the interviews within a fairly short period of time, perhaps two to three weeks. This enables you to maintain excitement, energy, and momentum. Designate a person or people from the Steering Committee to transcribe all of the interviewers' notes into one document. Give copies of the document to all Steering Committee members for reflection and analysis. Encourage the congregation to pray for the Steering Committee and the discernment process.

Step 4: Discern interview themes

The Steering Committee alone, or with the assistance of others, reflects upon the gathered data, and looks for shared themes. The Steering Committee asks questions. Where was leadership and participation optimal in the past? What were the key characteristics of those times and events? Where does the congregation want to go, and where do members perceive God is leading the congregation? Committee findings are presented to the congregation for review and input. The committee continues to keep the process positive and very public.

Step 5: Designing the future

The Steering Committee, staff, and others take the identified themes and restate them as goals, emphases, or ideals for the future. These statements are presented to the congregation council for approval, and referred to the appropriate committees for action and implementation. Again, the congregation is kept fully informed about how the interviews are being interpreted, and how they will be used as springboards into the future.

The design phase may be the most difficult for congregations. The Steering Committee has collected and analyzed all the interview data, and now provides new and renewing ways to apply it. Use creativity and innovation in the design phase to maintain the energy and enthusiasm of the AI process and make plans for the future.

Chapter 4 Tool

Gift Discovery for Individuals

Interview

Thank you for taking the time to be interviewed. I think you will find this to be a pleasant experience. All of the questions I ask will be related to how God has gifted you for ministry and service for others. Everyone is unique, and our congregation wants to know about your special needs and gifts. When we know what excites, motivates, and energizes you, we will be able to find ministry opportunities for you that are rewarding and that make a real difference in your life and in the lives of others. Do you have any questions or concerns? Let's begin.

1. Tell me about a time when you accomplished something that really made you proud. It doesn't have to be a "church thing." What made your accomplishment special? What made you proud?

2. Some people really enjoy working with other people on a team. Some people enjoy working alone. Which of those settings appeals to you most? In which setting are you most productive? Why?

3. Tell me about three skills or talents that you are glad you have. Don't be shy!

4. Tell me about three skills or talents you would like to strengthen or gain.

5. In what ways do you like to learn things—through reading, workshops, hands-on activities, classroom presentations, tapes, lectures, trial and error, with a mentor, all of these, or none of these?

6. When someone asks you to volunteer for something, how do you decide whether to accept or reject the request? Which requests do you accept? Why?

7. Some people are primarily interested in accomplishing tasks. Others are primarily interested in building relationships. Which interests you the most? Why?

8. Some people like to work primarily with their hands. Others are more interested in working with their heads. Still others want to use their hearts. Which of these best describes you?

9. Name some things you have always wanted to do or experience, but haven't yet done.

Checklist

Put a check mark by all of the following that apply to you. I enjoy and am skilled at or willing to learn:

__teaching	__child care	__youth ministry
__singing	__photography	__playing an instrument
__building things	__planning projects	__caring for seniors
__visiting	__goofing around	__dreaming up ideas
__public speaking	__cooking	__teaching the Bible
__playing sports	__carpentry	__drawing
__sewing	__creative writing	__organizing projects
__praying	__leading small groups	__finding volunteers
__office work	__creating artwork	__using computers
__gardening	__telephoning	__community building
__leading discussions	__nursery care	__making friends
__keeping things on track	__starting new things	__planning parties
__audiovisual work	__building consensus	__keeping things neat
__shopping for others	__solving conflicts	__talking about money
__acting and drama	__telling stories and jokes	__accounting
__inviting new people	__getting to know people	__typing
__meditating	__giving directions to others	

I think that I am called to . . .

I would really get excited if someone at church asked me to . . .

Name _____

Address _____

_____ Zip _____

Phone (day)_____ (evening)_____ Fax _____

E-mail _____

Chapter 4 Tool

Congregational Gift Inventory

Form small groups to reflect on the following categories and the ways God has blessed your congregation. You may want to work on the inventory individually and then share your results with the group.

Some of the congregation's gifts will be obvious, while others are not. Consider things that are problems or issues in the congregation. Could they also be opportunities and gifts?

When you have completed the inventory, discuss responses in the large group. Which gifts are shared and which are not? What does it mean that your congregation has been gifted in these particular ways?

Our people and leaders

(Examples: we have many elementary school teachers; Harold's work with stained glass)

Our financial resources

(Examples: our endowment fund; the youth group's fund raisers)

Our property and facility

(Examples: our well-maintained building; our location at a busy intersection)

Our neighborhood
(Examples: the local community organization; the new families moving in)

Our programs
(Examples: the AA groups that use our building; the women's circles)

Our structure
(Examples: we have several task forces; we have several effective committees)

Our history
(Examples: our traditions of hospitality and community service)

Our vision
(Examples: our goal-setting process; we have a compelling long-range plan)

Chapter 5 Tool

Motivation Self-Test

For each of the following statements you have three choices. Circle the one that best describes you. Choose only one answer for each statement. When you are done, add up the number of responses in each column.

	Column A	Column B	Column C
1. I think about...	people	problems	reputation
2. I give people...	comfort	my best	advice
3. I like...	friendships	challenges	winning
4. I dislike...	conflict	maintaining things	being led
5. I desire...	unity	innovation	status
6. People think I'm...	consoling	intellectual	powerful
7. Other people are...	fun	helpful	useful
8. I prefer...	group projects	clear objectives	giving directions
9. Conflict is...	uncomfortable	useful	necessary
10. I care about...	feelings	goals	influence
11. I like people who are...	warm/supportive	problem solvers	strong
12. I like to build...	communities	solutions	accountabilities
	Total _____	Total _____	Total _____

Key

The column with the most circled responses indicates your primary motivation type: Column A—Affiliation; Column B—Achievement; Column C—Power.

See pages 58-60 on McClelland's theory of motivation for more information on these types and the implications for congregations.

Personal Preferences

For each of the four categories, read each pair of words and place a check before the word that describes you best. Add the number of checks in each column. Write the letters for the higher totals in the blanks next to the category headings and in the boxes on page 103.

To learn more about the theory of psychological types, see pages 60-61 on the Myers-Briggs Type Indicator.

1. Focusing Attention _____

_____ lively	_____ calm
_____ talker	_____ listener
_____ loud	_____ quiet
_____ social	_____ private
_____ open	_____ withdrawn
_____ activity	_____ peace
_____ outward	_____ inward
_____ talkative	_____ reflective
_____ crowds	_____ alone
_____ trusting	_____ wary
_____ expressive	_____ reserved
_____ many friends	_____ few friends
_____ interaction	_____ solitude
_____ sociable	_____ shy
_____ people	_____ privacy
_____ **Extravert (E)**	_____ **Introvert (I)**

2. Gathering Information _____

_____ facts	_____ fiction
_____ reality	_____ fantasy
_____ details	_____ overview
_____ experience	_____ theory
_____ practical	_____ idealistic
_____ stability	_____ change
_____ traditional	_____ innovative
_____ cautious	_____ risk taker
_____ simple	_____ complex
_____ builder	_____ inventor
_____ realistic	_____ speculative
_____ present goals	_____ future goals
_____ satisfied	_____ ambitious
_____ specifics	_____ generalities
_____ practice	_____ improvise
_____ **Sensing (S)**	_____ **Intuitive (N)**

3. Making Decisions _____

_____ logical	_____ emotional
_____ firm	_____ gentle
_____ critical	_____ comforting
_____ hard-headed	_____ soft-hearted
_____ thinking	_____ feeling
_____ fair	_____ caring
_____ matter-of-fact	_____ romantic
_____ analytic	_____ sympathetic
_____ judge	_____ peacemaker
_____ contradict	_____ agree
_____ capable	_____ helpful
_____ impersonal	_____ personal
_____ rational	_____ irrational
_____ objective	_____ personal
_____ justice	_____ mercy
_____ **Thinking (T)**	_____ **Feeling (F)**

4. Using Time _____

_____ work	_____ play
_____ control	_____ freedom
_____ plan	_____ surprise
_____ scheduled	_____ unplanned
_____ careful	_____ careless
_____ plan ahead	_____ discover
_____ deadlines	_____ open ended
_____ organized	_____ unstructured
_____ finish	_____ start
_____ decisive	_____ curious
_____ arranged	_____ spontaneous
_____ deliberate	_____ impulsive
_____ structure	_____ independent
_____ decide now	_____ wait and see
_____ punctual	_____ leisurely
_____ **Judging (J)**	_____ **Perceiving (P)**

Your preferences: (1)   (2)   (3)   (4)

☐ ☐ ☐ ☐

Chapter 6 Tool

Ministry Description Form

Date _____

Ministry position title _____

Basic responsibilities _____

_____

_____

_____

_____

_____

_____

_____

_____

_____

_____

_____

Time needed to accomplish _____

Duration of commitment _____

Accountabilities (Who is in charge?) _____

_____

Goals to be accomplished _____

_____

_____

_____

_____

Training and support provided _____

_____

_____

_____

Evaluation and review provided _____

_____

Chapter 7 Tool

Sample Agenda
for a Leadership Retreat

Day One

6:30 p.m.	Refreshments, gathering time, conversation
7:00 p.m.	Opening worship
7:15 p.m.	Welcome, introductions, and announcements Sharing of the purpose of the event and mutual expectations
7:30 p.m.	Session One: "The Congregational Dilemma and the Disciple-Leader" (presentation and discussion based on chapters 1 and 2)
8:15 p.m.	Break
8:30 p.m.	Session Two: "Everyone is Gifted for Leadership" (presentation based on chapters 3 and 4)
9:00 p.m.	Small-group discussion
9:20 p.m.	Closing worship
9:30 p.m.	Refreshments, conversation, and community building

Day Two

8:30 a.m.   Morning worship

8:45 a.m.   Ice breakers and community building

9:00 a.m.   Session Three: "Gift Discovery for Individuals"
                 (working in pairs on chapter 4 tool)

10:00 a.m.   Break

10:15 a.m.   Group discussion, sharing of gift discoveries

11:00 a.m.   Session Four: "Individual Motivation and Style"
                 (presentation based on chapter 5)

11:15 a.m.   "Motivation Self-Test" and "Personal Preferences"
                 (individual work on chapter 5 tools)

11:30 a.m.   Small-group discussion regarding motivation and
                 personal preferences
                 Optional activity: Designate a corner or space for
                 each motivation type. Gather with others in your
                 type in the designated space. Discuss the advan-
                 tages and disadvantages of this motivation. Share
                 your insights with the large group.

Noon   Lunch

1:00 p.m.   Session Five: "Everyone Is a Disciple-Leader"
                 (presentation and discussion based on chapter 6)

1:45 p.m.   Break

2:00 p.m.   "Action Planning for Leadership Development"
                 (small-group planning based on chapter 7)

3:00 p.m.   Sharing small-group action plans
                 Discussion of next steps
                 Evaluation of retreat (Create a brief form inviting
                 feedback on the presentations and discussions,
                 suggestions for improvement, and topics the
                 group would like to explore further.)

3:15 p.m.   Closing worship (Note: The closing worship
                 could be based on the Affirmation of Baptism
                 service in *Lutheran Book of Worship*.)

Note: To allow the pastor(s) and congregational leaders to be active participants in this event, it may be helpful to invite someone from outside the congregation to lead the presentations and facilitate discussions.